Doing their Duty
England's rugby footballers helped win the First World War

PHIL MCGOWAN

PHIL MCGOWAN

Copyright © 2017 Phil McGowan

All rights reserved.

ISBN-13: 978-1546552727
ISBN-10: 1546552723

Acknowledgements- Thanks to Lewis Moody, Stephen Cooper and Mike Hagger for their assistance in the production of this work.

Thanks to the World Rugby Museum and to the Rugby Football Union for their ongoing commitment to the preservation and dissemination of rugby's rich and unique heritage.

Thanks also to that generation and men, women and children who fought and endured the Great War.   - Phil McGowan

Author's Note- This book has been written using a variety of sources including written memoires, personal diaries, letters from the front, medical records and regimental diaries. Where possible it includes quotes and direct references to the actions of the individuals involved. Other references are based on an assumed involvement in events in which the individuals' company, battalion or division were engaged. There may have been occasions when convalescence, leave or other unreported activity prevented this.

Contents

Forewords

The Declaration of War   p11

Readiness for War   p13

Rugby Union Footballers Are Doing Their Duty…   p15

    Jack King . Tim and Sos Taylor . Sid Smart

    Sammy Woods . Alfred Hamersley

1914

Battle of the Frontiers   p31

    George Dobbs

Digging In   p35

    Charles Wilson

Race to the Sea   p39

    Alfred Maynard

Naval Blockade and the War at Sea   p43

    George Lyon . James Watson . Frank Oakeley

1915

Naval Intelligence   p53

Stalemate of the Western Front   p54

    Percy Dale Kendall . Ronny Lagden

Bite and Hold   p61

    Fin Todd

Lost Generation   p65

    Ronnie Poulton

Poison Gas   p70

    Frank Tarr . Henry Berry

Defence of Suez	p77
Gallipoli	p78
Billy Nanson	
Suvla Bay Landings	p83
Arthur Dingle . Freddie Chapman	
Battle of Loos	p90
Geoffrey Dorling Roberts	
Hohenzollern Redoubt	p95
Danny Lambert . Harry Alexander	
1916	
Year of Battles	p101
Jutland	p103
Norman Wodehouse . Sydney Coopper . Dave Davies	
The killing fields of the Somme	p114
Bob Pillman . Tommy Voyce	
Wearing Down	p121
Noel Slocock	
The Rector of the Somme	p127
Rupert Inglis . Vincent Coates	
War of Attrition	p134
Robert Livesay	
Aftermath	p140
Len Haigh	
1917	
Revolutions: real and avoided	p144
Edgar Mobbs	
The Flanders Offensives	p151
John Raphael . Reg Pickles	
Passchendaele	p157
Arthur Wilson . John Ritson	

1918

Spring Offensives	p165
Battle of Lys	p169
Frank Mellish . Reg Hands	
The Flying Winger	p175
Cyril Lowe	
Naval Special Ops- The Zeebrugge Raid	p179
Arthur Harrison	
The Water Hen	p184
William Wavell Wakefield	
100 Days Offensive	p188
Harold Cecil Harrison	
General Tank	p193
Laurence Merriam	
The Armistice	p197
Reggie Schwarz	

I have always been fascinated by the First World War due to my Great Grandfather (Lewis Moody Senior) having been one of a small group of professional soldiers to set sail to France and Belgium with the British Expeditionary Force in the summer of 1914. Now, over 100 years later, we at least have an idea of the conditions that awaited them on the Western Front and my appreciation of he, and those who fought alongside him, grows as my understanding deepens.

The heroism of the likes of Arthur Harrison, who earned a posthumous VC for his role if the 1918 Zeebrugge Raid, is well known to English rugby fans but his story is one of many. From George Dobbs' crucial assistance in the retreat from Mons, to Lawrence Merriam's tanks breaching the Hindenburg Line in 1918, the more you trace the experiences of those men the more remarkable their stories become.

Edgar Mobbs was initially refused enlistment on account of his age but demonstrated his leadership qualities by returning with 264 men ready for service. Cyril Lowe was shot down in his observation plane in 1917 and so retrained and returned as a fighter pilot the following year.

Some, like Harrison and Mobbs, didn't return. Others, like seventeen year old Tommy Voyce, returned after fighting at the Battle of the Somme to earn their first England caps when rugby resumed in 1920. Phil's book describes how the actions of these men played out in the wider chaotic scenes of the First World War. It is a story of exceptional courage, bravery and achievement. It is also a story of ordinary men, doing extraordinary things, in the most trying of conditions.

Lewis Moody MBE

'Every player who represented England in rugby international matches last season has joined the colours', claimed The Times in November 1914. So they had, and 26 England men would die for their country before the final whistle four years later in November 1918; a twenty-seventh would die of illness in service soon after. This book deserves to be read, not only out of respect for those 27 men who left it all on the field, but also because their stories will now live after them through Phil McGowan's excellent work.

Stephen Cooper, Author 'The Final Whistle' and 'After the Final Whistle'.

'- history unparalleled... which will never be surpassed...history which will be held sacred by every Rugby lover for all time' – R.F Oakes[i]

The Declaration of War

The clouds of war had been gathering for many years before Britain formally declared war on Germany on the 4th August 1914. In the latter part of the 19th Century a series of European alliances had been forged in an effort to maintain a balance of power. Historically Britain had tried to stay out of internal European affairs but in 1904 took the decisive step of signing an 'Entente Cordiale' with France.

As the world's primary sea-power, Britain had then engaged in a naval arms race with Germany, as almost every other state in Europe jostled and bartered their way into one of two tidy blocks of enormous opposing factions bound together by treaties. Either of these blocks alone would have represented by far the largest stockpile of arms, naval and military equipment that had ever been assembled.

One of those opposing factions included the ailing Austro-Hungarian Empire, a multinational realm of different languages and cultures that included parts of modern-day Austria, Hungary, Ukraine, Moldova, Romania, Poland, Czech Republic, Slovakia, Croatia, Slovenia, Bosnia and Herzegovenia, Bulgaria, Serbia, Montenegro and Italy, all theoretically united under an autocratic monarch. It would be this region that supplied the trigger for war when, on the 28th June 1914, a Serbian nationalist called Gavrilo Princip succeeded in his second attempt to assassinate Archduke Franz Ferdinand, heir presumptive to the empire.

Even at this point very few expected 'the war to end all wars' and fewer still wished it. Austria wanted revenge against Serbia and sought the support of her German allies. This was duly granted even in the knowledge that Serbia would almost certainly look to Russia for help. Russia had a defence agreement in place with

France, who in turn could call upon the aforementioned entente with Britain.

Should there have been any doubt regarding British intentions they concerned the depth of her commitment to her allies. Britain had been intermittently at war with France for centuries and with her unrivalled navy and world empire, had traditionally stood aloof from European affairs, avoiding, wherever possible, becoming embroiled in the complicated power politics of the continent.

Germany herself might have preferred Britain as an ally but if one policy had served Britain well during the 19th Century it was the preservation of the 'status quo'. A unified European bloc under the command of Germany, who had already surpassed Britain in terms of industrial capacity, was definitely not in her interests.

Austria declared war on Serbia on the 28th July. Russia mobilised her army so Germany declared war on Russia on the 1st August and implemented the Schlieffen Plan. The Schlieffen Plan had been conceived by Field Marshall Alfred von Schlieffen in 1905. Its objective was to achieve a quick and decisive German conquest of France via Paris. In practice it involved a massive deployment of German troops into northern France partially by way of Belgium. Britain had been bound to defend Belgium by a treaty that was conceived in 1839 and so she declared war on Germany.

Readiness for War

The Royal Navy had for centuries been the main instrument through which the British Empire had been protected, serviced and sustained. By August of 1914 Britain had assembled the largest (by tonnage) fleet the world had ever seen, including 49 battleships, of which 29 were Dreadnoughts. The feared Dreadnought class battleships, introduced by First Sea Lord John Fisher, had 'reinforced the notion' that Britain had 'the most efficient and skillful naval systems in the world'[ii].

The Royal Navy would vie with Germany for supremacy in the North Sea and hoped their numerical superiority would allow them to enact a blockade on Germany's northern ports. Within her ranks were an abundance of English international rugby players, including 1914 Grand Slam winning side half-back partnership WJA Davies and Francis Oakeley, ably supported by James Watson and forwards Arthur Harrison and Alfred Maynard. Several more, including England's first Grand Slam winning captain Norman Wodehouse, Sydney Coopper and George Lyon were scattered throughout the fleet.

At the start of August the British Army numbered just under 250,000 regular troops[iii]. Amongst these were two full England internationals in the shape of Charles Wilson and George Dobbs. Wilson, a 43 year-old veteran, was an adjutant in the Queens (Royal West Surrey) Regiment who had seen action at the Relief of Ladysmith and Spion Kop during the Boer War. Dobbs was 30 and a second lieutenant with the Royal Engineers. Both had developed their rugby careers representing the Army before being selected for England. They would be amongst the first wave of soldiers to set sail for France.

Whilst Wilson and Dobbs were full-time professionals the regular Army also contained reservists and territorials. Amongst these, Henry 'Harry' Berry had first enlisted in 1899 at the age of sixteen. He had been decorated with the Gloucestershire Regiment but had never accepted a promotion[iv]. He had made his debut for England in 1910 in the inaugural fixture at Twickenham Stadium. Derbyshire's Frank Tarr, an imaginative three-quarter who had scored tries against France in 1909, was a lieutenant with the Leicestershire Regiment Territorial Forces and would soon be put to work as a machine gun officer[v].

Others were recalled from the Army Reserve. Robert O'Hara Livesay had played twice for England in the late 19th Century. During the Boer War he had received a Distinguished Service Order medal (DSO) whilst serving as a lieutenant with the Queens (Royal West Surrey) Regiment. He was recalled to duty in 1914 at the age of 38. Alexander Findlater Todd had earned two caps in 1900. He too had served during the Boer War and was recalled to the Norfolk Regiment at the age of 41.

In total Britain could mobilise almost 710,000 men[vi] but while some of these were kept at home, the greater part were already posted overseas meaning that just 100,000 men were ready for deployment as the British Expeditionary Force (BEF), that set sail for France in August 1914[vii].

'In every respect the Expeditionary Force of 1914 was incomparably the best trained, best organised and best equipped British Army which ever went forth to war' - Brigadier General J Edmonds[viii]

Germany however had mobilised more than 1.7 million men, with a similar number also having enlisted[ix]. The British Secretary of State for War, Lord Kitchener, correctly surmised that the war would be prolonged and that Britain would need more like 70 divisions and closer to 1 million fighting men[x].

Volunteers were therefore imperative to the sustainability of the British war effort.

Rugby Union Footballers Are Doing Their Duty…

'Rugby Football, to my mind, above all games is the one which develops the qualities which go to make good fighting men' - Admiral John Jellicoe, 1923[xi]

A symbiosis between rugby and the armed forces had already emerged by 1914. A game is thought to have been played at Balaclava In 1855, during the Crimean War[xii] and the Royal Engineers contributed two players, Charles Sherrard and Charles Crompton, to England's first international side in 1871.

The notion that the game had a capacity for instilling discipline and fighting relish in its participants was quickly taken up in a way that distinguished rugby from other sports. The United Services Rugby Football Club was founded in 1882 and both the Army and Royal Navy founded their own Rugby Unions in 1906. In recognition of their importance the Royal Navy, Army and latterly the Royal Air Force (RAF) were each given and have retained permanent representation on the Rugby Football Union (RFU) council.

It is therefore no surprise that rugby clubs were quick to respond to the crisis in Europe. Nine days after the outbreak of war the RFU issued a circular to its clubs advising all players to enlist with the armed forces. A month later on the 4th September they convened and decreed that in light of the 'supreme crisis' all club and county fixtures be cancelled, to be carried over to next season, 'all being well'[xiii].

> "This is not the time to play Games" (Lord Roberts)
>
> **RUGBY·UNION·FOOTBALLERS are DOING·THEIR·DUTY**
>
> over 90% have enlisted
>
> "Every player who represented England in Rugby international matches last year has joined the colours." — Extract from *The Times*, November 30, 1914.
>
> **BRITISH ATHLETES!**
> Will you follow this **GLORIOUS EXAMPLE ?**

The committee then discussed a proposal to organise a battalion of rugby footballers into a special Rugby Football Corps. It was rejected on the grounds of being too late since almost all rugby footballers were already inside barracks.

These remarks hint at the swiftness with which rugby footballers had responded to the call to enlist. The most famous recruitment poster of the war features Lord

Kitchener's pointed finger. The words- 'Your Country Needs You' solemnly informing all of their duty in Britain's hour of need. Another, lesser known, poster makes reference to the contribution of one sport as a beacon to all others.

A scrum-cap wearing colour illustration of a rugby player stands, square shouldered, with an England rose on his white jersey and a rugby football in his hands. Next to him another illustration of the same man, this time dressed in khaki tunic with shoulder straps and peaked cap, with a rifle in place of the ball. Emblazoned above 'RUGBY UNION FOOTBALLLERS are DOING THEIR DUTY over 90% have enlisted', below 'BRITISH ATHLETES! Will you follow this GLORIOUS EXAMPLE?'

The poster illustrates the sincerity with which rugby footballers answered the call to arms. Within twelve hours of the British declaration of war on Germany, Birkenhead Park FC, led by former England captain Percy 'Toggie' Kendall and another international and selector Jim Baxter, offered up her ground and pavilion to the war effort which was put to use as a recruitment centre[xiv]. Kendall returned to the King's Liverpool Regiment, known as the Liverpool Scottish, with whom he had served as long ago as 1900. Shortly afterwards the club reported to the RFU that they would not be able to fulfil any fixtures as her 'entire first XV' had also enlisted.

England's 'Pocket Hercules' of the 1913 season Jack King had been looking after his farm outside Ilkley when a chance encounter with a former teammate saw him enlist, almost at once, with the Yorkshire Hussars. His progress was checked however when after measuring he was found to be an inch too short for regulations.

King had once had to be physically prevented from returning to the field with two broken ribs for England in a game against Scotland in 1912[xv] and was not likely to be put off, ' I've come purposely here to join…and I'm simply going to stick here until you do take me in!' he said. Three days later a presumably exhausted recruiting officer relented and King signed his papers[xvi] leaving his sisters to run the farm. He would not remain with the Hussars for the duration however, later transferring to

Kendall's infantry regiment in order to see more of the 'action'.

Jack King

'None···have ever outshone Jack King in his love for this, the greatest of all games···' - R.F Oakes[xvii]

John Abbot King, the son of a cloth finisher, was born in Leeds in 1883. He was educated at Giggleswick School where he was introduced to rugby. In 1903 he moved to South Africa and furthered his rugby education by representing the fledgling Somerset West club on the Western Cape.

He returned to England and his native Yorkshire in 1906 to farm at Ben Rhydding on the eastern edge of Ilkley. He retained his love of rugby and established himself as a tough-tackling No.8, who thrived on being at the heart of the battle for Headingley RFC and then

Yorkshire, who he represented 46 times.

At just 5' 5" King was invariably one of the smallest players on the field but he more than compensated with a fearless mental resolve and reputedly a 45" chest[xviii], which earned him the nickname 'Pocket Hercules'.

He was first selected for England at the start of the 1911 campaign and embarked on a run of twelve appearances between 1911 and 1913. His work-rate and tenacity endeared him to the crowd and England would probably have secured a first Grand Slam in 1912 had King not suffered two broken ribs in the opening minutes of the game against Scotland at Inverleith.

In 1913 King had the opportunity to exact revenge against the Scots by helping England to a hard-fought 3-0 victory at Twickenham, a result that delivered England a Grand Slam for the very first time.

When King enlisted in 1914 he left his farm in the care of his three sisters. They inherited it when he did not return. Jack King died in 1916 and has no known resting place. He is remembered on the Thiepval Memorial and on memorials at Giggleswick School, Yorkshire County RFC, St George's Hall in Liverpool and St John the Evangelist Church in Ben Rhydding[xix].

Also amongst the roll call of the Liverpool Regiment were English forward Noel Slocock, Irish international Dick Lloyd and Scottish international captain Fred Turner, as well as Oxford blue and poet Noel Chavasse, who would become the only

serviceman to earn two Victoria Crosses in the Great War. With so many first class rugby players the Liverpool 1/10th Battalion is perhaps the closest to a 'rugby battalion' of all those that went into battle. It would distinguish itself magnificently.

Birkenhead Park wasn't the only club to turn its ground into a recruiting centre. Men across Leicestershire took the opportunity to join up alongside their mates in the so called Pals Battalions. 3,500 men joined the Leicestershire Regiment at Welford Road[xx]. Amongst these were the brothers Tim and Sos Taylor, the former of whom had earned an international cap against Wales in the opening game of the final championship before the war. His brother would be wounded within weeks of enlistment and then again so badly at the Somme that he was gravely informed that he would never play rugby again[xxi]. On the contrary he made his international debut against France at the war's end in 1920.

Tim and Sos Taylor

Tim and Sos were born Frederick and Frank in 1888 and 1890 in Leicester where they both attended Medway Street School. Whilst Tim was a technically gifted fly-half, Sos was a more robust prop and their shared love of the game spurred each other on as they progressed through Medway Old Boys, Medway Athletic, Leicester Tigers and Midland Counties.

During the 1913-1914 Season Tim received an invitation to play for England against Wales in the opening game of a campaign during which they hoped to defend the Grand Slam that they had won for the first time a year earlier. A close encounter followed but Taylor succeeded in freeing England's back-line sufficiently to secure a 10-9 victory that set the side on the way to repeating their feat of the previous season.

After the armistice Leicester were one of the first clubs to resume fixtures (in December 1918)[xxii] and both brothers returned to play. Tim was so highly rated that the side adopted a 'seven-forwards eight-backs' system in order to accommodate both him and Alf Bates. On the resumption of international rugby in 1920 Sos Taylor received an international call-up at the age of 29. Four years after being told he would never play rugby again he helped England to victories over France and Ireland.

Wasps, at the time based in Acton, West London, reported on the 21st of September that at least 92% of their members had 'joined the King's Forces in one branch or another'. In Gloucester, after Kitchener had made his appeal, a recruitment drive was held in the Shire Hall. The local *Citizen* newspaper recorded 'a tremendous cheer' going up as Sid Smart led a party of 300 into the colours of the Gloucestershire Regiment, amongst them most if not all of his cherry and white team-mates. Smart, who played at no.8 for Gloucester, had helped England to Grand

Slams in 1913 and 1914. Now he came to the assistance of his country with a company of Gloucester's finest men.

Sid Smart

Sydney Edward John Smart was born within a stone throw of Kingsholm. The son of a labourer he found work with the Gloucester Wagon Works soon after leaving school. In his spare he time he honed his skills as a fast and athletic No.8. By 1912 he had already established himself as a cherry and white regular and was selected for Gloucestershire, who he helped win the 1913 County Championship. His form didn't go unnoticed by the England rugby selectors and in 1913 he was one of five debutants at Twickenham selected to face the touring Springboks.

Smart became a mainstay of one of England's most successful sides, earning nine consecutive caps and helping England to back-to-back Grand Slams for the first time. He was twice wounded during the war and like Sos Taylor it was thought that his playing days were over. Like Taylor though he proved his doubters wrong by returning, first for Gloucester and then for England, to earn a further three caps in 1920. With him in the side Gloucestershire won the County Championship three times between 1920 and 1922.

Smart played his final season for Gloucester in 1923-1924 but remained in the town for the rest of his life. As a retiree he returned to the club as a steward and it was inside the grandstand that, at the age of 81, he finally passed away in 1969.

Northampton had their own champion in the shape of Edgar Mobbs, a veteran of 234 caps and 179 tries for the Saints and captain of England in 1910[xxiii]. The son of an engineer and a shoemaker, Mobbs was a formidable character who made a lasting impression on all he met. He offered to enlist as an officer immediately but was rejected, being deemed, at 32, too old. Undeterred Mobbs returned to Northampton and set about raising his own corps with whom he intended to enlist as a private.

Within three days the irrepressible Mobbs had raised 264 men whom he now presented, with himself at the front, to the recruiting sergeant for the Northamptonshire Regiment. Having demonstrated, so splendidly, his credentials as a leader of the type of men upon whom the British war effort would depend, Mobbs would not remain a private for long.

The age restrictions placed on recruits to Kitchener's Army would be lifted in time as necessity dictated but there were those, like Mobbs, who were not prepared to wait. Sammy Woods had torn holes in opposition defences whilst captaining England to a Triple Crown as far back as 1892. By August of 1914 he was 47 years old and suffering from varicose veins but was nonetheless determined to do his bit.

His first attempts to enlist were made in Wales where he was politely refused. He tried again and was refused again. Undeterred he left Wales to chance his arm in the Midlands where he was once again rejected on account of his age.

A fine disregard for the rules seems to have been a feature of Woods' make-up however and after speaking with a friend a place was found for him in the 6th Somersets. An old Victorian, Woods in his amusing memoirs describes his preparations for war as being as rigorous as his preparations for any other 'game' and compares the conditions in trenches as akin to his previous experience of 'wild-fowl shooting'[xxiv]. Eventually Woods was shipped off to Khartoum where he caught malaria. Mercifully the most serious injury he would suffer came when he fell down a drain after a long afternoon playing Bridge[xxv].

Sammy Woods

In a time when cricket was the summer sport and football the winter sport, Samuel Moses James Woods earned county representative honours in cricket, association football and rugby. Born in Sydney, Australia in 1868 he was sent to England to finish off his education at the age of sixteen. Soon after he formed a life-long bond with the county of Somerset and began playing rugby for Bridgwater as a versatile all-rounder who could kick, tackle and run.

He enrolled at Cambridge University where he earned multiple blues and in 1888 was called up to the touring Australian cricket side for whom he made his test debut against England. In 1890 he helped found Barbarians FC and received his call up for the England international against Wales.

England earned a share of the Home Nations Championship that year and Woods was described by a team-mate as running 'with the fury of a charging rhino' and by an observer as 'the most completely equipped of the English forwards of his time' [xxvi]. In 1892 Woods captained England during one of their most successful seasons on record, securing a Triple Crown without having conceded a single point. He earned the last of his thirteen caps in 1895.

In 1896 Woods toured South Africa as a member of the England cricket team. He remained in Somerset after the war and passed away in 1931 at the age of 64. He was posthumously described as Somerset's 'Godfather' [xxvii].

Schools made block contributions also. Three-quarter John Raphael, despite being a pacifist, had marched down with 60 Old Merchant Taylors to the headquarters of the Honourable Artillery Company to enlist. Of that club's 1914 first-team, thirteen would not return[xxviii].

Cyril Lowe and John Eric (Jenny) Greenwood were full England internationals and part of the so-called 'famous five' Dulwich College pupils who had gone on to become international rugby players. They also numbered among the 80 members of Old Alleynian FC, all of whom were reported by the school magazine to have enlisted. When Harlequins FC met for the annual general meeting most of them turned up in khaki[xxix]. Amongst their number England captains Adrian Stoop, Ronnie Poulton[1] and John Birkett.

In Oxfordshire the 128th, 132nd, 135th and 156th batteries were all recruited by a sexagenarian named Alfred St George Hamersley. The elderly but impressive Hamersley had featured in England's very first international back in 1871 and become the second man to captain England in 1874. Having recruited the men it would be reasonable to assume that Hamersley's work was done. Instead he took it upon himself to train them before pitching up in France himself in 1917 as a lieutenant colonel with the New Zealand Artillery at the age of 68. He returned the following year as the oldest England international rugby player to have served on the western front.

---

[1] Ronnie Poulton had by this point changed his name to Ronnie Palmer as a condition of a will inheritance. He is today often referred to as Ronnie Poulton Palmer although he never used this name. This book will use Ronnie's original name.

Alfred Hamersley

Alfred St George Hamersley was born in Great Haseley in Oxfordshire in 1848. He attended Marlborough College and began turning out for Marlborough Nomads as a powerfully resolute scrummager.

When the Rugby Football Union convened for the first time in 1871 his name was put forward for a place in the side that would represent England against Scotland in the first international football contest, held at Raeburn Place in Edinburgh. England and Hamersley lost on that occasion but were successful the following year. He featured in the draw of 1873 before captaining England to a second win in 1874.

Later that year he emigrated to New Zealand, having qualified as a barrister, and resumed playing rugby for South Canterbury FC, who he helped to establish. In 1888 he moved to Vancouver and became the city's first solicitor. He retained his interest in rugby and became the first president of the British Columbia Rugby Union.

In 1905 he retired back to his native Oxfordshire. Ever the missionary he set up the Oxfordshire Nomads RUFC in 1909, who later became Oxford RFC. He was elected as a Member of Parliament for mid-Oxfordshire in 1910 and passed away in 1929 at the age of 80.

These few hand-picked tales are representative of what was taking place in all corners of Britain as patriotic men, young and old, flocked to the banner. When the RFU formally cancelled all but school fixtures for the remainder of the season they

were simply echoing a decree that had been issued independently by rugby clubs up and down the country.

'To-day, every schoolboy must have read, and read, I am sure, with a great glow of pride, of that wonderful headlong rush the Rugby men made when the call to arms was sounded- when every "Rugger" club in the British Isles immediately closed its doors…" – RF Oakes[xxx]

The same was not true for all sports however. Professional team sports such as football and rugby league did not have the same flexibility with regards to fixtures and the release of players. Players held contracts with their clubs, the payment of which depended upon the receipt of gate revenues. Practicalities such as these determined how such sports were perceived and as losses began to accrue on the western front vitriol was aimed at 'shirkers' who pursued leisure while their countrymen fought and died.

'Every club which employs a professional player is bribing a needed recruit to refrain from enlistment, and every spectator who pays his gate money is contributing so much towards a German victory' – The Times, 17th November 1914[xxxi]

This presented a unique reputational coup for rugby union and an opportunity for recruiters who pointed out the perceived virtue of one game over another. George Rowland Hill, who had fought successfully to preserve the amateur status of rugby union in 1895, now saw justification for his fervent belief in the finer morality of amateurism. He derided his Football Association (FA) counterparts for having 'allowed one of the greatest sports in the world to be solely and entirely governed by commercial principles'[xxxii].

Rugby didn't stop entirely however. In fact almost as soon as the men were signed up they began organising games between units. These were encouraged by staff as a means to physical conditioning and of building and maintaining morale. Private Mobbs, who had been promoted to sergeant major and demoted back to sergeant within days of enlistment, had set about arranging and playing in a series of games against a Scottish Division, Welsh Division and the Barbarians at Hove, before setting sail for France[xxxiii]. It seemed that not only was rugby the sport of choice for the war effort it might even be the British Empire's secret weapon!

By mid-September Lord Kitchener's appeal had recruited almost half a million men[xxxiv] that included the fighting complement of English rugby. But as these new recruits were given over to barracks and basic training, other English international rugby players would find themselves caught up in the opening manoeuvres of the First World War as the British Expeditionary Force and French Army tried desperately to halt the German realisation of Field Marshall Alfred von Schlieffen's plan to secure the rapid conquest of Paris.

1914

Battle of the Frontiers

Fighting on the western front began in earnest on the 14th August with the Lorraine Offensives. For six days the French armies advanced, pushing the Germans back with considerable ease. But the German withdrawals were merely a stratagem, part of a well-conceived trap and on the 20th August, having succeeded in luring the French into isolated positions, their counter-offensive was launched.

The French, with their sabres, marching bands, bright blue coats and red trousers, were every inch a 19th Century infantry outfit. But tactics that might have served them well at Inkerman were about to be rendered hopelessly obsolete by German artillery and machine guns. The 22nd August 1914 was the single bloodiest day of the entire war. By marching his men in blocks across open terrain towards enemy gun emplacements French Chief of Staff General Joseph Joffre suffered the biggest single reverse in French military history- more than 27,000 killed in a single day's fighting[xxxv].

It was into this maelstrom, and on this day, that the British Expeditionary Force (BEF) arrived. Taking up a 20 mile stretch of front, part of which ran alongside the Mons-Conde Canal, five divisions dug in and awaited their orders. On the other side of the canal fourteen German divisions were approaching from the north[xxxvi].

Whilst the greater part of the British fighting force was still at home the BEF was about to make their stand. The Royal Engineers, with Lieutenant George Dobbs amongst their number, were ordered to sink the barges on the canal and lay explosives along the bridges. Dobbs, capped twice in 1906, was a signalman who would be tasked with maintaining lines of communication between east, west, artillery and HQ.

Just before midnight on the 22nd, a message was relayed to BEF Commander General John French from the French 5th Army requesting that they hold their position. French agreed. For the BEF the war was about to begin. They were now committed to the defence of Mons.

Like the French had done elsewhere the previous day, the Germans advanced as a block on the Mons-Conde Canal on the morning of Sunday 23rd August. The serene scene that awaited them was tribute to British positional concealment, but the hail of bullets that instantaneously cut down the most advanced German infantry painted a truer picture of what was to come. Machine gun emplacements had been placed along the line of the canal but it was their .303 Lee Enfield rifles, with their ten-round magazines, that the British would rely on to repel the enemy. As the only professional soldiers on the western front it was a source of immense pride to the British Army that their infantry were trained and able to fire fifteen rounds per minute at the very least, more than the enemy, and with greater accuracy[xxxvii].

Such claims were borne out by the events at Mons. The British held the line of the Mons-Conde Canal and inflicted three times as many casualties on the enemy as they suffered themselves[xxxviii]. As night fell however news came through that the French had fared less well. General Lanzerac had instructed his men to retreat, leaving the BEF at risk of encirclement. With the British flank about to be exposed Commander French had no choice but to order his men to fall back.

The following day the BEF withdrew, leaving a handful of manned gun emplacements along the canal with orders to repel the Germans long enough to allow the safe withdrawal of British forces. Lieutenant Dobbs remained at his post, relaying messages for long enough to ensure the safe withdrawal of both the British and French forces. For his action at Mons, the first English rugby international to see action on the western front became the first to be decorated. Lieutenant Dobbs was awarded the French Legion d'Honneur for his part in the withdrawal.

George Dobbs

Irish-born George Eric Burroughs Dobbs moved from County Kilkenny to England after winning a maths scholarship to Shrewsbury School. On leaving school he went to the Royal Military Academy where he was introduced to rugby football. A lithe forward who enjoyed running off the flank, Dobbs played for both Plymouth Albion and Devonport Albion before gaining representative honours for Devon.

In 1906 he received his international call-up to face Wales at Richmond Athletic Ground. Wales, featuring the likes of Gwyn Nicholls, Rhys Gabe and Dicky Owen, were Triple Crown holders but Dobbs acquitted himself well and was selected to face Ireland the following month. Later that year Dobbs toured Wales with the Barbarians and would feature for the Army in one of the very first Army v Navy matches in 1907.

Dobbs had enlisted with the Royal Engineers on completion of his studies in 1904 and was at the rank of lieutenant when hostilities commenced in 1914. Though the BEF were decimated, he survived until the penultimate year of the war. He is buried at Lijssenthoek Military Cemetery and his name is listed on the war memorial at Shrewsbury School[xxxix].

Digging In

Joffre's plan was to fall back and rely upon natural features such as the Ypres salient and the River Somme. Aware now of the nature of the German threat he preferred to stand and fight on ground most favourable to his cause. A fortnight of German advances followed during which the British and French were driven back towards Paris. By advancing the Germans sought to encircle and conquer the city.

Four additional British brigades arrived in September as the French moved their capital south from Paris to Bordeaux. By the 4th September the Kaiser received reports that his troops were within 30 miles of Paris. In accordance with Schlieffen's plan Germany had five days remaining to take Paris. After a fortnight of withdrawals Joffre decided that their stand would take place close to the banks of the River Marne.

The Battle of the Marne was fought 30 miles east of Paris, on land that turned from golden fields to churned earth as the heavy artillery did its work. There 36 Allied divisions, including Parisian reinforcements who famously travelled from the city by taxi, succeeded in halting the German advance.

On witnessing the BEF cross the Marne the Germans ordered a retreat that saw five of their armies fall back to a line behind the River Aisne. There they halted on a ridge that rose 500m to the north of the river and began to dig trenches. The BEF were amongst the first in pursuit, with 41 year old Adjutant Charles Edward Wilson, of the 1st Battalion Queen's (Royal West Surrey) Regiment, amongst their number.

Wilson had earned his solitary England cap against Ireland in 1898 and, like Dobbs, was a professional soldier and consequently had been amongst the first British troops to arrive in France. His regiment had served at Mons and now found itself close to Paissy Ridge in advance of the First Battle of the Aisne.

The River Aisne is deep and wide and only passable by bridging, therefore any Allied advance would be exposed to German artillery. Running low on horses and shells the 11th British Infantry Brigade were the first to attempt a crossing on the 12th September. They succeeded but found themselves under immediate enemy bombardment before ensconcing themselves on the crest of a hill[xl].

The Germans rapidly fortified their line of trenches with men and stores. On the 14th September, having gained a foothold north of the Aisne, Commander French ordered the British to do likewise[xli]. The pattern was now set for 'trench' warfare.

The Germans, holding the high ground of Chemin des Dames, were at an advantage in being able to train sniper fire and artillery at any infantry or stores that advanced in support of the British line and it was into precisely this terrain that Wilson was ordered to send his battalion.

On the 17th September his battalion crossed the Aisne. The artillery bombardment was predictably intense and Wilson himself was hit by a shell whilst bringing up the supports. Wounded he was removed from the battlefield but succumbed to his injuries several hours later. Charles Edward Wilson therefore became the first English international rugby player to lose his life to the conflict. Like Dobbs, he was awarded the Chevalier Legion d'Honour[xlii].

Charles Wilson

Born into a military family in Fermoy, County Cork, Charles Edward Wilson was educated at Dover College before enrolling at the Royal Military Academy in Sandhurst. By the time he had completed his training he was playing regular rugby for the Army and Blackheath Football Club. He toured with the Barbarians in 1895 and in 1896 was selected to represent the South in the annual North v South contest under the watchful eye of the England selectors.

Wilson's defensive work and contribution at the scrum helped the South win that game and another the following year. In 1898 he was one of six new players brought into the national side to face Ireland. Although Wilson acquitted himself well Ireland ran out narrow winners 9-6.

Three weeks later Wilson was back in action for the South but suffered a leg break after only ten minutes of play. The injury limited further involvement with the national side. Shortly thereafter Wilson served in the Second Boer War, taking part in the Relief of Ladysmith, the Battle of Spion Kop and the Battle of Tugela Heights. He was awarded the Queen's Medal with two clasps and the King's Medal with two clasps for his service.

He is buried in Paissy Churchyard close the River Aisne where he fell.

Race to the Sea

In response to the stalemate at the Aisne and the ferocity of enemy artillery and gunfire both sides now chose to dig in. A solid line of trenches and impenetrable natural defences stretched from the Swiss border to Verdun and now the Aisne. Attention quickly shifted north and west as both sides attempted to outflank the other in search of an opening. The race to the sea had begun.

As a series of encounters stretched the front-line north through Picardy, Albert and Arras, the British Admiralty switched its attention to Belgium. The Germans occupied Bruges and Ghent and on the 28th September began an assault on the city of Antwerp. First Lord of the Admiralty Winston Churchill feared the loss of Antwerp would open the way to western sea ports from whence an assault and possible invasion of Britain might occur and so he moved to defend the city.

By August of 1914 the Royal Navy had a surplus of 30,000 conscripts[xliii]. Unable to find sea-going billets for so many, the men were converted into a land division, initially called the Royal Naval Division. Amongst these new recruits was Alfred Frederick Maynard, known to his team-mates as 'Freddie', he had debuted for England earlier in the year. In contrast to Dobbs and Wilson, Maynard was just 20 years of age and, caught up in the patriotic fervour of the summer, set aside his final year at Cambridge University in order to enlist[xliv].

Antwerp was defended by multiple perimeter forts and 80,000 fortress troops in addition to the Belgian Field Army and government who were stationed there[xlv]. On the 28th September the Siege of Antwerp began. Out of the range of Belgian guns, the enormous German Howitzer 'Big Bertha' siege guns began to lay waste to the Belgian forts while above German zeppelins dropped their payloads on the city.

The following day the Belgian government announced their intention to withdraw, along with the Field Army, to Ostend and appealed to Britain and France for assistance in the defence of Antwerp. Joffre was unmoved but Churchill answered the call.

More fortresses fell as the German's tightened their noose around the city. Churchill himself arrived with the first of the naval brigades on the 4th October. Maynard's brigade arrived two days later and made an audacious attempt to evade the German bombardment and fortify the city's remaining inner forts. They succeeded and proceeded to defend the city for a further four days under fierce fire from the German heavy siege guns.

Eventually, with German advances threatening to completely encircle the defenders, they were ordered to withdraw. With the city ablaze and now in enemy hands, three battalions of the Royal Naval Division, 'Hawke', 'Benbow' and 'Collingwood', found themselves cut off and were forced to abscond into the Netherlands where they became military internees[xlvi].

Maynard's 'Howe' battalion however was able to escape across the Scheldt on the evening of the 8th October. The city's inhabitants, also in the process of fleeing, were held back as they crossed. From the west bank of the river Maynard would have seen the city lit up like an orange ball against the night's sky. Antwerp had fallen and over 60,000 Belgian soldiers had been taken prisoner or fled north but the Howe Battalion would fight another day[xlvii].

Alfred Maynard

'...a veritable giant of a man, full of life and good humour...' – H. B. T Wakelam[xlviii]

William John Maynard, Alfred's father, had featured for England in the first international association football contest in 1872. Alfred Frederick, sometimes known as Freddie, however would prove more adept at the oval ball game and captained Durham School as a teenager before going up to Emmanuel College, Cambridge in 1912. He gained rugby blues that year, alongside Cyril Lowe, and the following year when he ran half the length of the field to score a try, his thick limbs being reportedly difficult to stop once allowed to build-up a head of steam[xlix].

In between terms he turned out for Harlequins and Durham City before being asked to represent Durham County as a hooker. His meteoric rise through the representative ranks continued when, at the age of just nineteen, he was selected to help England defend her Grand Slam and Triple Crown honours at the start of the 1914 season.

A useful addition to the English line-out and a workhorse in the scrum Maynard did precisely that by helping England to wins over Wales, Ireland and Scotland before injury prevented his involvement in the season finale in Paris. He would undoubtedly have earned further caps had the war not intervened later that year.

He died in 1916 and is remembered on the Thiepval Memorial in the valley of the Somme.

By the 19th October the meandering line of the western front was established and with it the end to any lingering hopes that the war might be over by Christmas. Entrenched defensive positions on both sides heralded stalemate, and trench warfare meant that future battles would be resolved over weeks and months, not hours and days. Attempting to look on the bright side Commander French described the situation to his wounded men as a 'stalemate in our favour'[1]. The war of attrition had begun.

Naval Blockade and the War at Sea

Britain had maintained her naval superiority in the years before 1914 by constructing enormous iron-clad ships called Dreadnoughts with colossal twelve-inch guns. When war commenced she had 29 of these ships to Germany's eighteen[li]. As a result Germany kept her capital ships in port where they would be protected by coastal defences.

Britain's primary naval objectives were containment and blockade. The Grand Fleet was stationed at Scapa Flow in the Orkney Islands from where it was hoped she could patrol the 155 miles between Scotland and Norway. Likewise a contingent of armoured cruisers and submarines were to keep the German High Seas Fleet out of the relatively narrow English Channel. In this way Britain would blockade German ports and restrict her access to the outer seas.

Within weeks of the declaration British naval command had formulated a plan for an audacious raid on German patrols in their own coastal waters that resulted in the Battle of Heligoland Bight. The plan was to cut off and attack a complement of German destroyers returning from night patrol.

The raid would be led by Vice Admiral David Beatty from the HMS *Lion*. On his bridge was Arthur Leyland Harrison, a square-jawed lieutenant commander and front-five forward for the Royal Navy, United Services and England. Harrison had been in the thick of two English victories earlier in the year, against Ireland at Twickenham and France at Stade Colombes, now his battlecruiser would be at the thick of the opening salvoes of war at sea with Germany.

Around midday on the 28th August *Lion* and four battlecruisers plotted a course through the gun smoke and fog in support of an embattled British destroyer. An officer on board the smaller vessel described their arrival as akin to 'elephants walking through a pack of dogs'[lii]. Shortly afterwards *Lion*'s mighty guns sank the SMS *Ariadne* and SMS *Coln*, inflicting the most grievous losses of the day and thus ensuring the success of the action.

Heligoland Bight cost the Germans six ships in total and effectively neutered the High Seas Fleet in the early phase of the war. For the rest of the year German fleet operations would be mostly limited to mine-laying and U-boat manoeuvres. But German U-boats would pose a significant threat in their own right as the British would soon discover.

At the start of the war British submarines outnumbered German U-boats by 55 to 28[liii]. A German U-boat, *U15*, had been sunk as early as the 8th August, just four days after war had been declared. The U-boat had opened fire on a British battleship, the HMS *Monarch*, whose Gunnery Officer George Lyon was a former English international captain and full back. HMS *Birmingham* had then proceeded to ram and sink the U-boat ensuring it would not return from its maiden voyage.

George Lyon

George Hamilton D'Orly Lyon was born on the Indian subcontinent in 1883. He was educated at Bruton School and the Royal Naval College at Dartmouth before joining the Royal Navy in 1899 at the age of just fifteen. Not long after he was making waves as a full back for both the Navy and United Services.

A contemporary, John Raphael, said of him- 'Lyon's whole-hearted methods were delightful to watch, and made him a pleasing figure on every football field' [liv]. At the end of the 1908 international season an injury crisis saw him receive his international call-up to face Scotland at Inverleith. A close encounter followed in which the home side eventually prevailed. Lyon however had done enough to be retained and was chosen to captain the side the following year against Australia at Blackheath.

Lyon's international career ended with two caps. He played first-class cricket in the years before the war and married Helenora in

1912. He was promoted to the rank of commander in 1918 and had risen to vice- admiral by 1938. He was commander-in-chief, The Nore in 1941 before retiring in 1943. He passed away in 1947 at the age of 63.

Though most British submarines were designed for shallow coastal use, the Admiralty did have a small contingent of deep water submarines, three of which had been present at the Battle of Heligoland Bight. On board HMS *D2* was England half back Francis Oakeley.

Lieutenant Oakeley was one of Britain's first submariners as well as an outstanding, quick thinking scrum half. He had helped England to back-to-back Grand Slams in 1913 and 1914. Unmarried and aged just 23, Oakeley maintained a steady stream of correspondence with his mother in Torquay, with whom he had lived before the war.

The threat posed by German U-boats would be brought into sharp perspective by the events on the 22nd September in an area of the North Sea called the Broad Fourteens. A single German U-boat, the SMS *U9*, intercepted a trio of armoured British cruisers on a routine patrol and sank them all in less than an hour[iv].

The lack of appreciation of the U-boat threat at the time is evidenced by the response of these British ships. Light cruisers could easily outrun surfaced U-boats but instead of taking evasive action, the second and third ships went to the aid of first U-boat target, thus condemning their own ships to the same fate as the one they were seeking to assist. All three cruisers were sunk with a loss of 1,459 lives. In response new directives were issued regarding the U-boat threat. From now on ships were expected to retreat in a zig-zag pattern that would allow them to avoid the devastating torpedoes.

But these sensible new directives would not help another member of England's 1914

Grand Slam side. James Watson, was serving on the HMS *Hawke*, another North Sea armoured cruiser engaged in routine patrols. Watson, an attacking three-quarter, had scored against France in Paris earlier in the year and had enlisted as a surgeon at the war's outbreak. On the 15th October, *U9*, the very same lone German U-boat that had wreaked such destruction at the Broad Fourteens intercepted *Hawke* as she lagged behind the rest of her convoy. A torpedo dispatched *Hawke* without warning. Adhering to the new directives HMS *Theseus* took evasive action instead of attempting to rescue her crew[lvi].

Eventually 70 survivors were pulled from the wreckage but Watson was amongst the 524 who were not[lvii]. Thus James Watson became the first English international rugby player to lose his life at sea during the First World War.

James Watson

James Henry Digby Watson was born in Southsea in 1890. He first began playing rugby as a pupil at King's College, Canterbury and later at the Edinburgh Academy where he was transferred in 1906. He gained the nickname 'Bungy' when asking his Scottish classmates for a rubber eraser using the slang of his former school in England.

He progressed to Edinburgh University to study medicine and surgery. There he represented Scotland at the long-jump and became the university's middleweight boxing champion. By 1912 he had established himself as the captain of Edinburgh Academicals RFC and his rapid darts from outside centre had begun to catch the eye of selectors on both sides of the border.

He toured Wales with the Barbarians in 1912 and was chosen as a reserve for Scotland the same year. After moving south he played for Blackheath FC and London Hospital.

England, the country of his birth, selected him in 1914. His debut came in a narrow victory over Wales at Twickenham. Later that season he returned to Edinburgh with England and helped them to a narrow 16-15 victory, securing the Triple Crown in the process.

Watson's final cap came against France in the last international before the war. It was a resounding success with Watson himself crossing the try-line in a 39-13 victory that delivered England consecutive clean-sweeps, or Grand Slams as they are now known.

He is remembered on memorials at King's School, Edinburgh Academy, Edinburgh University and Blackheath FC[lviii].

The precarious nature of life at sea was further illustrated the following month.

Lieutenant Oakeley had been half way through writing a letter to his brother when he had been called to operations on his submarine, *D2*. On the 23rd November, *D2*'s captain was swept overboard amidst rough North Sea squalls. Oakeley assumed command and after trying unsuccessfully to find his lieutenant commander, returned to port.

Two days later, with a new lieutenant commander in post, *D2* set out again. This time they were destined for the mouth of the River Ems, where Oakeley and the sub had been present at the Battle of Heligoland Bight. On reaching Borkum Island they detected a German torpedo boat and surfaced in order to engage. The German boat however was ready for them and proceeded to ram them[lix].

The impact caused Oakeley's submarine to sink with the loss of all on board. His unfinished letter to his brother, in which he pledged to visit him in Canada should he be 'alive and kicking after this show', remained unsent in his room in Harwich.

Frank Oakeley

'…swift, nimble and highly intelligent.'   - A.A Thomson[lx]

One of eleven children, Francis Eckley Oakeley attended the Cathedral School in Hereford before joining the Royal Naval College at Osbourne on the Isle of Wight. He completed his training at Dartmouth in 1908 before entering the fleet as a midshipman at the age of seventeen.

He played his rugby as a scrum half for Portsmouth, the Navy and the United Services and his accurate passing and work-rate saw him form a useful partnership with fly half Dave Davies. Wins were secured in the Army v Navy matches of 1912 and 1913 before the Davies-Oakeley partnership was called on to replicate its naval successes for the national side. Oakeley earned his first cap for England in the final game of the 1912-13 season, against Scotland at Twickenham.

Victory in this game gave England the Triple Crown and meant that they had achieved a clean sweep of victories for the first time since France had become the fifth member of the 5-Nations Championship.

The following year both Davies and Oakeley were replaced for the season opener but a narrow victory against Wales forced the selectors into a rethink and both returned for the following game against Ireland. The decision was vindicated when the half back pairing sent the English backs over the try-line five times.

Four more were scored against Scotland before England put nine past the French in the season finale to deliver a second consecutive clean sweep. In just four caps Oakeley had helped England to back-to-back Grand Slams and was credited by ER Ward of the Morning Post with having upheld the chivalric example lain down by the likes of George Lyon[lxi].

Francis Oakeley was 23 at the time of his death. He has no known grave and is remembered on the hand written memorial board of St Mary's Church in Cockington[lxii], and another at St Matthew's Church in Chelston.

1915

Naval Intelligence

1915 opened with a breakthrough at the Admiralty. With the assistance of the Russians and Australians Britain had developed the means to intercept and interpret German naval instructions. A group of cryptanalysts, code-named 'Room 40' after the room from which they operated, set to work deciphering German naval transcripts. In this way they learnt of an imminent German offensive at Dogger Bank in the North Sea.

The Germans had recently launched coastal raids on Scarborough, Hartlepool and Whitby and hoped to attack the British fishing fleet. The Admiralty sent a larger squadron to intercept them with HMS *Lion* once more to the fore. Having learnt of the deaths of Watson and Oakeley, with whom he represented England in Paris just a few months earlier, Lieutenant Commander Harrison must have hoped for the opportunity to redress the balance.

The Battle of Dogger Bank began at 8.00 on the 24th January when three German battlecruisers came within sight of *Lion*. Of five British battlecruisers she was the first to engage and shortly afterwards landed a direct hit on the turret of the German flagship SMS *Seydlitz*. The explosion ripped through the ship's ammunition chamber, taking out both turrets for the loss of 165 lives[lxiii].

The remaining ships now engaged and SMS *Blucher* came under sustained fire that left her disabled. The other German ships abandoned her to her fate and headed for port. *Blucher* was sunk with a loss of almost 800 lives. Despite her victory *Lion* had sustained serious damage during the encounter and limped back to port before undergoing months of repairs. Lieutenant Commander Harrison would play no further part in the campaign until she returned.

Stalemate on the Western Front

'…our men have played and are playing the game. We are still in the scrum, it is true, but the ball is being carried forward, and we doubt not that in God's good providence the goal for which we are fighting – the goal of freedom, justice and lasting peace – will soon be won.' – Colonel Treeby[lxiv]

With trench lines established, and the earth growing hard in the cold of winter, both sides sent reinforcements to strengthen their positions on the western front. The first of Kitchener's volunteers had begun to arrive in Belgium and France in October of 1914. Amongst this first wave were Toggie Kendall, who had rallied his men so effectively at Birkenhead Park, and Alexander Findlater Todd.

Alec 'Fin' Todd had been a burly forward for Rosslyn Park, Blackheath, England and the side that would one day be known as the British and Irish Lions, as far back as 1896. A professional soldier, he had fought as a squadron commander during the Boer War and signed up for the operations in France at the age of 41. He had been mentioned in despatches by the end of 1914 and promoted from lieutenant to captain with the Norfolk Regiment 1st Battalion, who found themselves engaged in the winter defence of Ypres. In November he wrote a letter to his ten year old daughter, thanking her for sending him winter underwear and describing, 'sitting out in the snow for three days and nights…as shooting was going on all the time'[lxv].

The harsh realities of trench warfare were now coming to the fore. The First Battle of Ypres was in fact a succession of battles, as both sides prodded and poked the enemy line for signs of weakness. None were found. Unable to outflank each other, all progress would depend on frontal attacks in which attackers would come under sustained rifle and machine gun fire. Todd's regiment and the remainder of the BEF were resolute in their efforts.

It quickly became apparent that trench warfare would favour the defending force. Although the BEF suffered a loss of 58,000 men at the first encounters at Ypres, effectively decimating their ranks, the Germans lost as many as 130,000[lxvi].

Germany was forced to acknowledge that the plan for a rapid conquest of France was at an end. Instead they quietly began withdrawing men from the western front for redeployment in the east, trusting their machine guns to hold the line in their absence. As the German strategy switched to one of containment the onus would be on the Allies to eject them, thus the defensive advantage passed over to the invaders.

Five miles south of Ypres, Toggie Kendall's Liverpool Scottish 1/10th Battalion arrived in Kemmel and immediately occupied front-line trenches. Like Todd, Kendall had been swiftly promoted and was now a second lieutenant. His battalion however was subjected to heavy fire from both machine guns and snipers.

The sniper threat had initially been under-appreciated by the British. Not so the Germans, who attached scope lenses to their rifles and began putting them to deadly use, offering cash rewards for the killing of British officers[lxvii]. It would be some months before British forces discovered one of these weapons and made the connection between them and the high numbers of reported deaths by 'ricochet'.

The gunfire and appalling conditions in the trenches took a heavy toll on the Liverpool regiment. Of the 850 men who arrived with the Liverpool Scottish 1/10th Battalion, only 370 remained by the start of February 1915[lxviii]. Sadly amongst the fallen was their second lieutenant. Kendall was hit and killed by a 'ricochet' bullet on the 25th January[lxix] becoming the first former England captain to give his life to the conflict. The high casualty rate amongst officers during the First World War is well documented and in 1915 snipers did much of the work. Kendall was 35 when war broke out and was under no compulsion to enlist, but had done so within twelve hours of the declaration.

Percy Dale Kendall

'On her playing fields he served his country, on her battlefields he died.' - F.C.H[lxx]

Percy Dale Kendall was born in Prescot, Lancashire in 1878. He attended Elleray and Tonbridge Schools before enrolling at Cambridge. In between he developed as an exciting and vocal half back for his club, Birkenhead Park, and for Cheshire, who he represented on 45 occasions.

Whilst training as a solicitor he played for Blackheath FC and was later selected for the Barbarians. He received his full international call up for the first time in 1901, against Scotland at Rectory Field.

In his second cap his half back partnership with Bernie Oughtred ran the Welsh close, leading with minutes to go before the Welsh snatched victory with a late penalty. His final cap came against Scotland in 1903 when he led his team-mates out at Richmond's Athletic Ground as captain.

Known to his team-mates as 'Toggie', he is remembered on club memorials at Birkenhead Park and Blackheath as well as at Tonbridge School and St Andrew's Church in Bebington[lxxi]. He left a wife and two children.

As losses began to mount, the need for reinforcements became apparent. In the first months of 1915 Kitchener's appeal began to bear fruit as thousands of volunteers arrived in France and Belgium. Amongst these were many of the English internationals who had so decisively answered their nation's call to duty the previous summer.

Harry Berry, who had served in South Africa, India and Ceylon before playing alongside Edgar Mobbs, Ronnie Poulton and Leonard Haigh in Twickenham's inaugural 1909-10 season, arrived with the Gloucester Regiment 2nd Battalion in February of 1915. His Gloucester team-mate Sid Smart of the Gloucester Regiment 1/5th Battalion arrived with his men the following month. Back home in Gloucester the recruitment drive continued and a seventeen year old auctioneer's clerk by the name of Anthony Thomas Voyce signed up. He would arrive in France with the 2/5 Gloucester Battalion in 1916.

Harold Hodges with the Monmouthshire Regiment 3rd Battalion also arrived in February, 1915. Ronnie Poulton, England's Grand Slam winning captain of 1914, arrived with Royal Berkshire Regiment in March. So too did Frank Tarr with the Leicestershire Regiment 1/4th Battalion.

Most of these new arrivals were eager to reach the front and put into practice the skills that they had spent the long winter months acquiring. A different sort of monotony awaited them however as they began the rotation between front, reserves and short leave. The majority at least would not see battle for several months but fate had determined a different course for Captain Ronny Lagden of the King's Royal Rifle Corps 6th.

As part of the Rifles 4th Battalion the Richmond, Oxford and England back was ordered to take up a position in the trenches outside the rural village of St Eloi. As little as 30 feet separated the Allies from the enemy here and intense skirmishing took place throughout February and March, leaving the British short of men. If the Rifles 4th thought that they were there to make up the numbers they were mistaken. Captain Lagden was given just days to familiarise himself with the terrain before receiving orders that he was to lead 300 men in a frontal assault on the German trench opposite.

The full implications of such an order would not have been lost on the intelligent young captain. Regardless he carried it out to the letter. After ordering his men over the top he personally led the charge from the front. MG machine guns awaited and 113 of the 300 men quickly became casualties. Inevitably Lagden was amongst them. When asked if he would return he instead ordered his men to advance and, incredibly, returned to his feet and advanced with them. Already badly wounded he walked on into the bullet storm and eventually succeeded in reaching the enemy trench. He was last seen lying wounded atop the parapet.

Lagden's father had once written of rugby:

'So, it is up to every boy at every school which is a nursery for new generations of Internationals to remember that there is in Rugby football something noble that counts for more than winning goals and points'[lxxii].

His Commanding Officer later acknowledged that Lagden's 'task was an impossible one' but that the captain of D Company did 'all that was humanly possible to carry it out'[lxxiii].

His date of death is recorded as the 3rd March 1915. In Edward Sewell's 1919 Roll of Honour he wrote:

'Lagden's must have been a fighting finish, game and true to the last breath, a glorious example to generations of Rugby men and Britons yet to come.'

Ronny Lagden

Ronald Owen Lagden was born in Basutoland in modern Lesotho in 1889. He attended Marlborough College and Oriel College, Oxford where he immersed himself in multiple sporting disciplines such as hockey, rackets, cricket and rugby.

Between 1909 and 1911 he earned multiple blues as a lock in a team that also featured Ronnie Poulton and Bruno Brown. In 1911 he joined Poulton and Brown in the national set up when called into the English pack to face Scotland at Twickenham. England won the match and Lagden, who had also played half back, demonstrated his versatility by converting two of England's three tries. An injury to the knee prevented further caps but Lagden continued to play for Richmond.

Captain Lagden has no known resting place. He did not marry and his name is recorded on the Menin Gate, Ypres[lxxiv].

When the conflict was over his father wrote:

'Our Rugby game has given of its best…The sacrifice is great, but they were the men to offer it – those who had learned to play the game of Rugby Football and loved its ethics' – G. Lagden K.C.M.G, 1919

Though Lagden's brief contribution to the war was inspirational in its heroism and bravery, the action at St Eloi was ultimately futile and is blackly illustrative of the capacity for slaughter that trench warfare entailed. This was to be a war unlike any that had been fought before. It was clear already that breaking the impasse would require either colossal loss of life or radical new strategies.

Bite and Hold

New strategies were attempted in the spring of 1915. Reinforcements continued to arrive and went some way towards mollifying French fears over the British commitment to the war effort. Until now Kitchener had hoped that France and Russia might do most to contain Germany but by doing so he ran the risk of defeat. The action of Neuve Chappelle in March 1915 was conceived partly to demonstrate British commitment and partly to try and find a way to break the fortifications on the western front[lxxv].

A 'creeping barrage' of 300 heavy guns focused their attack on a mile-wide stretch of German front and succeeded in breaking it, allowing the Allies to take and hold the village and road. The successful tactic wasn't fully appreciated however and the British were reluctant to advance further, allowing the Germans several hours to send reinforcements. On arrival they learned more of the British success than the British themselves and ironically it was they who subsequently made the most of the tactic on the Eastern Front against the Russians.

A new type of warfare was also taking place underground. Hill 60, a mound of soft earth that had been piled up during the construction of the Ypres-Comines railway line, lay on the south-eastern edge of the Ypres Salient. It was known locally as 'Côte des Amants' or 'Lover's Knoll' and in early 1915 five mines were dug underneath the hill by the British tunneling companies who quietly placed explosives directly below German positions opposite.

On the 17th April, England captain Ronnie Poulton, sat and watched the night's sky light up with violent flame from the safety of the Belgian town of Romarin. Of the five mines below Lovers Knoll, two had been detonated. The Battle of Hill 60 had begun.

Captain Todd had been fighting on the salient when the Germans had taken the hill back in November and he and his regiment would now play its part in recovering the high ground. A series of massive explosions painted the night's sky red and succeeded in decimating the German defences. The British, with Todd's Norfolk Regiment in the vanguard, then overwhelmed the stricken Saxon Infantry Regiment and seized the German trenches.

The following morning the Germans launched a series of three massive counter-attacks on the hill. A monumental defensive effort by the Norfolk Regiment and others repelled them and ensured British control of the hill for the time being at least. Captain Todd however had been caught by a bullet through the neck.

At first his wounds were not thought to be life-threatening and he was taken away to a dressing station. Though he had been spotted smoking a cigarette as he left the battlefield his wounds were worse than first anticipated. He had registered his brother as his next-of-kin so that his wife Alice should not be first to receive any sad news[lxxvi]. He died three days later leaving a wife and two children. 'In respect of her late husband' Alice would apply for one of his medals five years later in 1920.

Fin Todd

Alexander Findlater Todd was born in Lewisham in 1873. He was a scion of the Findlater, Mackie & Todd wine merchants who would be absorbed by Waitrose supermarket in the 1990s. He attended Mill Hill School before enrolling with Caius College, Cambridge where he achieved three consecutive blues for rugby between 1893 and 1895.

On leaving university he sailed off with the 1896 British team to South Africa. A tall, burly marauding forward he drew comment from observers for his size and physicality. Early Lions tours were as much a social as a sporting occasion but pack leader Tom Crean introduced strict regulations whereby Todd and the other players were restricted to just four glasses of champagne before competing on the field[lxxvii].

Such limitations didn't hold Todd back however and he featured in four test-matches against South Africa, scoring a try in the second and winning three in total. On return he joined Blackheath from

Rosslyn Park and in 1900 was selected alongside Harry Alexander to represent England against Ireland.

The semi-frozen pitch may have reminded Todd of the hard pitches of the Cape but tight scrummaging saw England to her first win in two years and first against Ireland in five. Todd retained his place in the side and fought out a tough 0-0 draw with Scotland at Inverleith as England finished a respectable second in the Championship table.

Later that year Todd was back in South Africa as squadron commander in the Boer War. He was wounded at the Battle of Diamond Hill.

He is buried in Poperinghe Old Military Cemetery and his name is listed on memorials at Mill Hill School, Caius College, Blackheath, Rosslyn Park and All Souls' Church in Ascot[lxxviii].

Lost Generation

In Romarin, Ronnie Poulton, the England captain and possibly the most famous rugby player in the world at the time, would have received the news of Todd's death with great sadness. Since the war's outbreak he had lamented the loss of so many of his friends, writing in the News of the World that 'England in defending her honour will have to face the loss of the very best of her sons[lxxix]'.

Remembered as a dashing, swerving outside-centre whose elusive running had brought England no fewer than four tries when sealing the 1914 Grand Slam in Paris the previous year, he was now known as Lieutenant Palmer of the 1st/4th territorial battalion of the Royal Berkshire Regiment.

He had arrived in France on the same ferry *Onward* that had taken him and his team-mates to that Championship decider in Paris less than a year ago[lxxx]. This time, dressed in Khaki, with standard military moustache, he would represent his country under different circumstances. He and his men had been stationed on the front-line at Ploegsteert Wood, called Plugstreet by the British.

Much is made of the 'lost generation' who gave their lives to the Great War. Poulton, like so many others, was warm, humorous, thoughtful, intelligent and well regarded by his team-mates and men. He was also socially conscientious in a way that set him apart. In the two years before the war he had been learning his trade amongst the engineers at Mather and Platt's firm in Manchester. He was enormously popular and his plain and honest manner allowed him to gain the trust of both workers and management at a time when industrial tensions were particularly high. On receiving his inheritance of the Huntley and Palmer biscuit factory (which necessitated his name change) Poulton immediately began setting out his plans for workplace reform and for improving welfare provision for his workers[lxxxi].

Before sailing for France he had taken the time to send 250 Christmas parcels to the children of his co-workers in Manchester[lxxxii]. In his short life he had demonstrated an unusual degree of political subtlety and it is likely that, had he lived, he would have contributed more fully. His brother noted his admiration for the response to war from conservatives and the church[lxxxiii] but in his letters to his sister he expressed views that would have been shared by many of his men. The war, he said had rendered him a 'hide-bound socialist' and he credited international socialism as the only thing that might prevent it[lxxxiv].

In April 1915 his company was set to work making night-time improvements to the defences of the trench emplacements at Ploegsteert. In his journal and letters Poulton records coming under machine gun fire and shelling, which he described as 'very frightening…the nearing whistle and then the burst, and then you wonder if you are alive'[lxxxv].

Sniping was the constant daytime threat and in a letter to his father he described the Germans having 'absolute superiority' of the sniping within the sector but expressed a confidence that there was no danger of sniping in the evening by way of 'mutual agreement I suppose'[lxxxvi].

Shortly after midnight on the 5th May 1915 Poulton was shot under his third rib whilst standing on top of a dugout in Trench 40. His belief that a mutual understanding would prevent night-time sniping is indicative of his faith in humanity. He was also not aware that German snipers were given free license to roam the front-line. Reputed to be amongst his final words were 'I shall never play at Twickenham again'.

On hearing the news of his death a friend lamented his loss:

'He felt very strongly on the utter folly of civilised nations resorting to such methods for the settling of their differences, but above all he felt that by going to a war from whence he would probably not return, he was shattering at a blow all those hopes of being of some real use to humanity in the future. His potential value to the nation was so great that he should not have been allowed to go'[lxxxvii].

Ronnie Poulton

Ronald William Poulton was born in 1889 and attended Dragon School in Oxfordshire before going to Rugby School and then Balliol College, Oxford. His proficiency as a rugby player was noticed whilst he was still at school and in 1909 he was capped for England at the age of nineteen, before he had even been selected for Oxford University.

An explosive outside centre whose mazy runs bewildered his opponents and excited spectators he quickly became integral to Adrian Stoop's exciting back division at Harlequins FC, with whom he played in Twickenham's inaugural fixture in 1909. Later that year he scored a record five tries for Oxford University in the Varsity Match against Cambridge University.

In 1910 he played in Twickenham's first international fixture and helped England to a first win over Wales since 1898. A first outright Championship since 1892 followed. His first try for England came in 1912 and in 1913 he was one of his side's chief attacking threats in a season that would deliver England her first clean-sweep of the 5-Nations era.

In 1914 Poulton was installed as the England captain. The honour spurred him on to his most complete performances as a rugby player. In England's final game before the outbreak of war Poulton scored four tries against France to hand his side a second consecutive Grand Slam.

In 1913 and 1914 Poulton worked as an apprentice engineer at Mather and Platt's factory in Manchester and played several times for Liverpool FC. In 1914 he inherited the Huntley and Palmer biscuit factory. A condition of the inheritance was that he adopt the name 'Palmer' and he is now often referred to as Ronnie Poulton Palmer despite never having used the double-barreled surname.

He is buried at Hyde Park Corner in Belgium and remembered on memorials at Rugby School, Oxford Univeristy RFC, Balliol College and Liverpool FC[lxxxviii]. Many have said that he was the finest player of his generation.

'A beautiful player, a character of the highest integrity, one of 'the loveliest and the best. With his fair hair and fleet limbs, he might have stood as a symbol at the heart of England, of Rupert Brooke's generation, of the golden young men who died faithfully and fearlessly in a war where much that was of value beyond price in an imperfect world perished, too.' - A.A Thomson[lxxxix]

Poison Gas

Despite being a signatory to the 1899 Hague Convention which prohibited its use, Germany added a terrible new dimension to the war on the western front when, in April of 1915, it released 168 tonnes of chlorine gas at Gravenstafel Ridge, thus triggering the Second Battle of Ypres.

Chlorine gas, once in the lungs, produced water effectively causing the inhaler to drown. It sowed immediate panic amongst the Allies, who were initially unsure of how to negate its killing properties. Driving home their advantage the Germans pushed the Allied line back until they had taken the town of St Julien. Having done so they brought their heavy artillery up into a position from where they could strike at the 27th and 28th British Divisions who were holed up on the exposed Frezenburg Ridge.

Harold Hodges' Monmouthshire Regiment was caught up in the fighting as part of the 83rd Brigade, who made up the 28th Division. French-speaking Hodges, a former schoolmaster from Tonbridge School, had played for Nottingham, Oxford University and England as a muscular prop-forward. Earlier in the month he had written to his mother commenting on his dislike for the 'whizz-bang' light artillery that approached his men with little warning. He also expressed a sense of the creeping fatigue that accompanied the series of disappointments that had so far typified 1915.

'We are anxiously awaiting a really great piece of good news from the outside world, we have had nothing these last few days, though rumours abound, e.g that the passage of the Dardanelles has been forced and a big fight of Norway, how one longs for the war to be over…'[xc].

The regiment's trench positions were well within range of German heavy artillery. As the sun rose on the morning of the 8th May 1915 a colossal artillery bombardment was brought to bear on their position decimating the 83rd Brigade and effectively ending Hodges' battalion as a fighting force. Hodges himself had been hit by a shell earlier in the battle and had been withdrawn before the worst of it. His wounds were described as severe but he would return to the front just two months later with several pieces of shrapnel still in his body[xci].

Hodges' Oxford University team-mate and Leicester Tigers' star player Lieutenant Frank Tarr was less fortunate. His Leicestershire Regiment battalion were holed up in dug-outs close to Lake Zillebeke. As acting-adjutant he had taken up an advanced position to consult another adjutant when they came under direct shelling. Their shelter received a direct hit and Tarr was killed by a splinter that hit him in the head. He had been recommended for promotion to captain[xcii].

Frank Tarr

Francis Nathaniel Tarr was born in Ironville, near Belper in Derbyshire. He attended Stoneygate School, then Uppingham before enrolling at University College, Oxford in 1906. A fast distributor and sound tackler Tarr earned his first blue in 1906 as an attacking centre three-quarter.

As well as playing for Oxford University he turned out regularly for Leicester Tigers, where he went to work as a solicitor, and in 1908 was selected to play for England against Australia alongside George Lyon and Edgar Mobbs.

Within three minutes, intricate passing between himself and Mobbs had resulted in the games' first try. He played against Wales at Cardiff Arms Park and France at his home ground- Welford Road in Leicester. The game saw nineteen year-old Ronnie Poulton earn his first cap but it was Tarr who stole the show, scoring two tries and helping England to a 22-0 victory.

Later that year Tarr played alongside Poulton in the Varsity Match in which the latter scored five tries. Tarr's final cap for England came in 1913 at Twickenham against Scotland with England needing to win to ensure their first clean-sweep of the 5-Nations era. Win they did, by the narrowest of margins and Tarr had added his name to the list of England's first ever Grand Slam winners.

Tarr is buried at Zillebeke, Belgium, close to where he fell. He is remembered on memorials at Welford Road, Uppingham School, Oxford University RFC and Richmond Athletic Ground[xciii].

At the same time as the Germans were attacking at Ypres the French and British were mounting an offensive in the Second Battle of Artois. Harry Berry, who had at last accepted a promotion to the rank of corporal, was with the Gloucestershire 2nd battalion. They had been involved in the defence around Ypres and now found themselves moved to new positions from where they could assist the British offensive at the Battle of Aubers Ridge.

If ever there was a doomed First World War offensive it was this one. With almost no artillery support, the British attempted a frontal assault over open ground towards two lines of reinforced German machine gun emplacements. Many were shot in the act of going over the top. Those who were able to advance discovered that thick coils of barbed wire remained in place around concrete German bunkers. Those who survived the initial firestorm were reduced to digging into artillery craters to escape the relentless pounding of the enemy guns[xciv].

A private from Corporal Berry's section later described how they each shook hands and kissed photographs of their wives and children before clambering over the top of sandbags and charging headfirst into the maelstrom on the 9th May 1915. 11,000

British casualties were recorded on that single day without making so much as a dent in the German line. Berry was one of several hundred from his regiment who did not return. Precisely 100 years (to the minute) after he and his Gloucester teammate Harry Barnes had made their final fatal rush, fans of Gloucester RFC broke off from watching their side play London Irish at Kingsholm to stand and applaud their courage.

Henry Berry

Henry Berry, more often known as 'Harry', was one of nine children born to a dock worker in Gloucester. He left St Mark's School at the age of fourteen and in 1899 enlisted with the Gloucester Regiment militia volunteers. During his time in uniform he served in South Africa, Sri Lanka and India and developed an interest in rugby.

He joined Gloucester RFC in 1907, initially as a wing. Although fast he was also strong limbed and his transformation as a player came when he was convinced to play as a wing-forward. In 1910, after impressing in the trials he was selected to play for England against Wales in Twickenham's inaugural international fixture.

Berry's rapacious tackling helped England to record their first victory over Wales in twelve seasons. He was selected again to face Ireland and was one of only a handful of players retained again to face France. The selectors' faith in him was repaid when he forced his way over the French line for the game's opening try.

In the final game of 1910 season Berry scored again, this time against Scotland, at Inverleith. He was one of only four players to feature in every round of England's first championship winning season since 1892.

Later that year Berry played in the county championship final for Gloucestershire against Yorkshire. He played 135 times for Gloucester in total. He married Beatrice in 1910 and the two of them ran a pub in Gloucester. His son Henry was born in 1911. A month after Berry's fatal charge at Aubers Ridge Beatrice gave birth to a daughter, Phyllis Irene.

He is remembered on Le Touret Memorial, Pas de Calais, at Kingsholm and at St Mary de Lode Church[xcv].

When GD 'Khaki' Roberts of Harlequins and England arrived at Festubert later that year he gravely and graphically observed that the rats had grown 'fat and sleek' on the unburied corpses of those who had perished in the battle[xcvi]. Smaller actions

around Flanders continued over the summer of 1915 and on the 27th July British infantry captured the village of Hooge. With the 7th Rifle Brigade was a 21 year old lieutenant called Laurence Merriam who had played as a lock for Oxford University. Three days later the Germans introduced a new and terrifying weapon to the western front in the shape of the flamethrower, which engulfed British troops with jets of burning gasoline. The appalling weapon spread significant apprehension amongst the ranks of the British but Merriam and his company nonetheless succeeded in capturing and holding a line of forward trenches inside a mine crater. In defending the position Merriam was hit by a trench mortar. He was badly injured but escaped with his life. The following year he was drafted into the newly formed Machine Gun Corps and would return in time for the Battle of the Somme.

Defence of Suez

For all of the occasional horror of the Western Front the overall picture remained one of stalemate. But elsewhere there was potential for change as new entrants to the war threatened to alter the balance of power. By January 1915 70,000 Allied troops had amassed in Egypt[xcvii]. The reason for their presence was the strategically vital Suez Canal that linked naval operations and trade in the Mediterranean with the Red Sea and subsequently the Indian Ocean. Egypt and the canal had been under the protection of the British since the 1880s but was a target for the Ottoman Empire who had officially sided with the Axis-powers the previous year.

British fears were well founded and on the 26th January the Ottoman Turks launched an audacious raid from the eastern bank of the canal. The Allies however were well prepared. In order to attack the Turks had had to march 25,000 men across the Sinai Desert. Throughout the war the British had been at the forefront of a series of technological developments and early in the war employed light aircraft as spotters. Inevitably the advancing Turks had been sighted by reconnaissance aircraft and, although fighting lasted a week, they were easily repelled for minimal losses.

Alfred Maynard and the Royal Naval Division had been unable to prevent the fall of Antwerp but he and the Howe Battalion at least shared in the successful defence of Suez. His next involvement in the war would be markedly different. Despite the war having already demonstrated that machine guns favoured defenders over attackers, the Admiralty was about to go on the offensive.

Gallipoli

In January 1915 Russia requested Allied diversionary attacks against the Turks to relieve pressure on their own forces, at the Caucasus Mountains in particular[xcviii]. The ease of the victory at Suez and some small naval victories elsewhere perhaps convinced First Lord the Admiralty Winston Churchill that easy gains might be had against the Ottomans. As stalemate persisted on the western front, plans for an additional front in the east began to ferment. The result was the Gallipoli Campaign.

The narrow straits of the Dardanelles and Bosphorus, either side of the Sea of Marmara and Turkish city of Constantinople (now Istanbul), links the Mediterranean with the Black Sea. Britain had benefited from the straits and the restriction of movement placed on the Russian Black Sea Fleet for much of the 19th Century but now the boot was on the other foot. A failed minesweeping operation in the mouth of the Dardanelles in March convinced First Sea Lord Fisher that the straits were impregnable. Instead they would land on the long Gallipoli Peninsula. In taking the sea ports of the Dardanelles by land, they hoped to open up a route to Constantinople.

On the 25th April under the cover of darkness, Alfred Maynard's ship approached the peninsula's narrowest point, near to Bulair and little over 5km from the Sea of Marmara. At first light the convoy began a bombardment of the coast line that would last most of the day until late in the afternoon when Maynard and the rest of his division boarded landing craft and headed for the shore. Once they were within a few feet of the beach they stopped. As darkness fell they turned their craft around and quietly returned to their ships.

Their approach had been one of two feints designed to divert attention away from the main attacks that were taking place elsewhere. During the night Lieutenant Commander Freyburg, a former rugby player with the San Francisco Barbarians, had swum ashore and noted that the Bulair landing was largely undefended[xcix].

The same was not true elsewhere. After returning to their ships the RND were transported south-west to assist with the landings at Cape Helles. At 'w' beach, Turkish defenders had dug trenches in the sand and placed barbed wire right down to the water's edge. On landing the Lancashire Fusiliers had been subject to direct fire from rifles and machine guns within 100 yards of the beach. Of the 950 that tried to land, 500 were shot. In his report their major described a sea that 'ran crimson'[c]. In a monumental effort that famously won '6 VCs before breakfast'[ci] the Lancashires succeeded in securing the beach and moved inland.

Similar resistance awaited the Hampshire Regiment and Royal Munster Fusiliers at beach 'v' and the indomitable ANZACs who had landed further north in an inaccessible cove that would afterwards be renamed in their memory. Contained within their ranks former Northampton, British and Irish Lions and Australia forward Blair Swannell would lose his life, like so many others, in an advance on the fortified hilltops.

At beaches 'x', 'y' and 'z' the landers had taken the beaches without contest. Their campaign objective was to take the inland village of Krithia and, after the initial landing, Marine Lieutenant Commander Mathews was able to walk to the village unopposed[cii]. Had an order to advance been received at this point the village might have been taken with minimal losses. It wasn't and instead the Allies would spend the rest of the year engaged at Krithia.

The Allies lost 4,000 men during the landings and a further 3,000 during the First Battle of Krithia three days later, which confirmed that the defenders had reinforced their positions. Reinforcements were found in the shape of Maynard's Royal Naval Division and the 42nd Division, amongst whom the 10th Battalion (Oldham) Manchester Regiment included William 'Billy' Nanson, a former Rugby League professional who had been capped for England in the amateur code twice in 1907.

Like Maynard, Nanson had been stationed in Egypt during the defence of Suez. He landed at Cape Helles on the 9th May, a day after the Allied forces had been repelled with heavy losses at the Second Battle of Krithia. As wounded men were brought down to the beach and onto hospital ships, replacements such as Nanson were sent in to take their place in trenches on the western edge of the village, only a few metres separating them from Turkish positions[ciii].

Maynard and Howe Battalion arrived the following day and joined Nanson outside Krythia. On the 19th May the Turkish forces launched a counter-attack on the ANZAC positions. It was repelled but Maynard took a bullet to the leg and joined the snaking line of casualties down to the beach. Fortunately for him his wound was treated and he was evacuated to Alexandria.

Sergeant Nanson also come under heavy fire from snipers and artillery and with diminished strength the Oldhamers were drafted into the 29th Division and prepared for an assault on the Turkish trenches on the 4th June. The Third Battle of Krythia would introduce the horror of the western front to Gallipoli and prove beyond doubt that matters on the peninsula were in a similar state of stalemate.

Lieutenant Bleakley described a 'veritable hell on earth' as Nanson went over the top. Of the 188 men in D Company only four returned. Nanson was last seen heard shouting 'come on lads, lets shift'em' as he went to clean-out an occupied Turkish trench[civ]. His body was never recovered and his wife Margaret and two young children Marjorie and Charles would have to wait another thirteen months before his death was declared officially[cv].

Billy Nanson

William Moore Bell Nanson was born and raised in the shadow of Carlisle Rugby Football Ground. The son of a slater he attended Lowther Steet School before joining the Border Regiment, with whom he served and was decorated for his role in South Africa during the Boer War.

On his return he joined Carlisle RFC as a stalwart forward and is recorded as being 'a tower of strength' to the club[cvi]. He represented his county and was selected for the North of England in a 1906 trial match against England, which the North won. The following year he was called up to the national side to face France.

He was one of seven internationals to make his debut, others included Danny Lambert and Noel Slocock. England ran riot. Lambert scored five tries, a record for a debut, while Nanson added one of his own. But Nanson's second cap was as disappointing as his first was encouraging, Wales comfortably dispatching their visitors in Swansea by six tries to none.

In 1908 Nanson, now a father of two, joined the professional ranks of the northern union and played Rugby League for Oldham, Coventry and Todmorden before becoming a full-time slater like his father.

He has no known resting place and is remembered on the Helles memorial in Gallipoli and the civic war memorial in Oldham[cvii].

Suvla Bay Landings

Successive failures on the peninsula saw Churchill removed from his position in the Admiralty in May 1915, but the British government was not yet ready to wind up the whole campaign. In what historians would later describe as 'lunatic persistence in the face of the obvious' [cviii], it continued with an expansion of the front in the summer of 1915.

Two divisions were mustered for landing at Suvla Bay on the 6th August, in their ranks a 23 year-old lieutenant, known to his former team-mates as 'Mud' Dingle. Though only 23 Arthur James Dingle had founded the Officer Training Corps at Durham School before his enlistment in August of 1914. Earlier the same year a run from his own half had set-up Ronnie Poulton in England's Grand Slam winning contest with France in Paris.

Lieutenant Dingle landed with the East Yorkshire 6th Battalion, nominally a pioneer battalion, but one that would find itself involved in almost everything at Suvla. Like at Bulair and initially Anzac Cove, the bay had only minimal defences in place. Despite this Dingle's battalion came under fire during the landing and secured the beach and nearby hillock, only after sustaining significant losses.

Although the entire British chain of command had acknowledged that the primary 'initial' aim was to secure the bay itself[cix], the wider campaign would be decided by whether the landing parties could achieve what had not been achieved at Anzac Cove, fortifying the heights before Turkish reinforcement could arrive.

Only Dingle's battalion came close to realising this when a company of the East Yorks 6th approached Tekke Tepe on the 9th August. Lieutenant Still later wrote of having arrived on the summit of a hill that was 'key to the whole position' and of having found it to be undefended[cx]. The company however was isolated and reinforcements didn't arrive until the following day where they were greeted by four Turkish field guns that tore into the 32nd Division, igniting the dry shrub land and causing the scattered retreat of what little remained of the division[cxi].

In a letter to his father Dingle described 'a perfect hailstorm of bullets' during 'the most terrible day one could imagine'[cxii]. In the general disorder he and his men had abandoned nearby Scimitar Hill after receiving a delayed order to advance on Tekke Tepe. Scimitar Hill offered the opportunity to link the troops at Suvla with those at Anzac. Having reacted too slowly to the opportunity at Tekke Tepe, British command now threw away what gains they had made. Days later Scimitar Hill would be the site of the largest battle of the whole campaign.

In between, Dingle described the condition of his *battalion* '…we have suffered very heavy casualties, only 6 officers left and about 280 men out of 700'[cxiii]. With so few officers remaining Dingle was given command of the 150 men of B Company.

The 11th Division's attempt to retake what they had abandoned came after an artillery barrage on the 21st August. They succeeded only to find that the hill was exposed to Turkish gun emplacements higher up. In a classic display of Englishness, newly gazetted Captain Dingle, finding himself in one of the most advanced trenches and under constant fire, chose not to retreat but instead to make tea for his men[cxiv].

The following morning brought Turkish counter-offensives and given the officer casualty rate at Gallipoli it is perhaps not surprising that Dingle was one of the first to be shot. He continued to direct his men, reportedly even after receiving a bullet to the head, but when his men withdrew they did so without him.

Lieutenant Still who had been taken prisoner at Tekke Tepe ten days earlier, wrote expressively about the events of Suvla Bay during his captivity and included the following epitaph for the young lieutenant from Sunderland.

> Broad and simple, and great of heart,
>
> Strenuous soul in a stalwart frame;
>
> Whatever the work, he took his part,
>
> With energy strung from the very start
>
> To learn the rules and play the game.
>
> He played for an English side before;
>
> And all unspoiled by the crowd's applause,
>
> He took for his side their greeting roar:
>
> And so in the greater game of war
>
> He gave his life for the greater cause.

Arthur Dingle

Arthur James 'Mud' Dingle was born in Hetton-le-Hole in 1891. After attending Durham School he enrolled at Keble College, Oxford where he earned a blue in 1911 alongside Ronnie Poulton and Ronny Lagden. Both Poulton and Dingle scored tries, helping Oxford to a 19-0 victory.

Later that year he represented the North against England and also played regularly for Rosslyn Park and Richmond FC. On completion of his studies he returned to County Durham to work as an assistant master and put his powerful, fast runs from inside and outside centre to use for Hartlepool Rovers, whom he captained in 1914.

In 1913 he would rekindle his centre partnership with Ronnie Poulton, this time for England, against Ireland in Dublin. A vintage England side won by 15 points to 4 and Dingle's name was added to the select group of players who delivered England her first Grand Slam. The following year he repeated the trick. This time, playing on the wing, he assisted England to a narrow win against Wales and a merciless nine try demolition of France in the final international game before the war.

Dingle's body was never retrieved from Scimitar Hill. His name is recorded on the Helles memorial and memorials at Durham School, Keble College, St Margaret's Church, Durham; St John the Baptist Church, Egglescliffe; Richmond FC, Rosslyn Park FC, Hartlepool Rovers and Oxford University RFC[cxv].

By the time the East Yorkshire 6th reconvened on the beach they were down to just four officers and 250 men. Those who had been evacuated with injuries were taken offshore to the hospital ships where their wounds could be treated by the Royal Army Medical Corps, with whom was another Twickenham hero. Like Maynard and Dingle, Freddie Chapman was from the north-east of England. A surgeon by profession, he worked tirelessly treating the wounded in the hospital ships of Suvla Bay and would have received the news of the loss of his Hartlepool team-mate Dingle with great sadness.

As the summer turned to autumn, then winter, Captain Chapman's workload intensified. The wounded kept coming and were joined by those suffering from dysentery and frostbite as conditions worsened. Eventually the order was given by Kitchener to evacuate the peninsula. This was completed in early January of 1916. For all the efforts of its combatants the campaign was a costly failure that incurred 205,000 Allied casualties[cxvi]. However the campaign did succeed in one primary objective. By opening up the Gallipoli front the Allies *had* relieved the pressure on the Russian infantry in the Caucasus.

Freddie Chapman

Frederick Ernest Chapman played alongside Mud Dingle for Hartlepool Rovers and was remembered long afterwards for his clever touch-line trickery and side-steps off either foot. Having attended South Shields High School he went to Durham University where he trained as a surgeon.

He could play on either wing, in the centre or at full back. In between representing Durham County he was selected to tour Australia and New Zealand with the 1908 Anglo-Welsh side (an early progenitor of the British and Irish Lions). He scored eight tries in twelve appearances.

In 1910 he upset the apple cart by helping a 'Rest of England' side to defeat England comfortably on the eve of the opening fixture of that year's 5-Nations Championship. As a result he was one of a number of players parachuted in to the England team to face Wales in the very first international fixture to be played at

DOING THEIR DUTY

Twickenham Stadium.

Within 30 seconds of kick-off Chapman had made history by becoming the first man to score an international try at Twickenham. He followed that up by becoming the first to kick a penalty and then a conversion in helping England to a first victory over the Welsh in twelve seasons. Three caps later he had helped England to a first outright Championship victory since 1892.

He earned the last of his seven international caps in 1914, kicking two vital conversions that helped England to a 10-9 victory over Wales in a season that would deliver a second consecutive Grand Slam.

Despite being twice wounded he returned to county rugby with Durham in 1919. He passed away in 1938 at the age of 50.

Battle of Loos

Despite Gallipoli the Russians fared badly on the eastern front throughout 1915 and in September Tsar Nicholas II took a personal gamble by assuming control of the Russian war effort. The stalemate in the west had facilitated German progress in the east and the Anglo-French 1915 autumn offensives were conceived to redress the balance.

Earlier events in 1915 had made clear that carnage awaited any frontal attack on reinforced German lines. Nonetheless Kitchener instructed his Field Marshal to accept 'very heavy losses indeed' to assist the offensive[cxvii]. The British advance would take place along a nine mile stretch of industrial landscape that included miner's cottages, railways and slag heaps, north of the town of Loos.

The Battle of Loos would begin on the 25th September. Edgar Mobbs and his self-raised company of men within the 7th Northamptonshire Regiment had marched 60 miles by nightfall in order to take part. Mobbs, on enlistment, had been promoted to sergeant-major but had requested a demotion to Sergeant so that he might remain with his men. This had been granted but failed to halt Mobbs' meteoric rise through the ranks and one year later Captain Mobbs landed in France as the Commanding Officer of D Company[cxviii].

Mobbs' battalion came into the 24th Division who would constitute the second wave. Further ahead Second Lieutenant GD 'Khaki' Roberts and the 8th Devonshire Regiment were stood ready as the first wave of the assault. Their objective was to overrun the first line of German trenches and progress west. The Germans however had built a second deeper line, fortified with concrete machine gun emplacements called 'Stutzpunkt', either side of the Devonshire's route. Further north the

Hohenzollern Redoubt was a defensive strongpoint flanked by machine guns on a rise overlooking a wide flat across which Mobbs' division would later advance.

In his memoirs Roberts' recalls the air 'filled with the strange sounds of the passage of the invisible harbingers of death, the rustling of the heavies mingled with and drowned by the tearing screams of the high velocities'[cxix]. Vividly describing the feeling of exposure that must have gripped many of the men gathered under the trench parapet at Loos he describes a 'feeling of complete nudity caused by the hiss and whine of the occasional bullet'[cxx].

A similar feeling must have gripped Roberts as he stood waiting for the whistle to be blown but with minutes to go his company received an unexpected order- 'No battalion is to take more than 20 officers into action'[cxxi]. As a second lieutenant, he was amongst those stepped down and ordered to observe the line of attack from the rear. The events that he subsequently witnessed would be recalled later that day in Advanced Brigade HQ as a 'tale of gallantry and appalling slaughter'[cxxii].

His company commanding officer, alongside whom Roberts would have led the charge, received six bullets to the legs shortly after going over the top[cxxiii]. Britain had used chlorine gas for the first time in the assault at Loos but lack of wind meant that it had not reached German trenches and in some cases had wafted back towards Roberts' battalion[cxxiv]. Despite this they overran the German front line and made further progress until they came in range of the Stutzepunkt.

Seeking to make good the gains, Mobbs' company and the 24th Division were brought up in support. The Hohenzollern Redoubt had been taken and they took up positions well in advance, which they occupied the next day when Roberts too was also ordered up in support.

At first light Roberts crossed no-man's land and found the remnants of the 8th Devonshires in a forward position called Gun Trench. On his way there he described 'the stillness of death' and the 'carnage of the battlefield…smashed transport, abandoned equipment…horses, some dead, others maimed'[cxxv].

His battalion had been reduced from 750 to 130 men. Furthermore, to his self-described horror, he was the most senior officer and therefore assumed command of what was left of the battalion. In the afternoon 10,000 men, including those of Mobbs' division, advanced on the German second line only to be mown down in their thousands. Those that reached the line found the wire uncut. Having reached it the British columns were obliged to turn around and retreat. The situation was so dire that reports suggest the Germans ceased fire out of compassion, appalled at the losses they themselves had inflicted at a place they would later describe as the 'corpse field of Loos'[cxxvi].

Mobbs' had so far escaped the carnage and was preparing a counter attack when his trench came under bomb attack. He was wounded but refused to be evacuated. Instead his company stood their ground, holding the position for the remainder of a day that Mobbs described as being 'like all hell let loose'[cxxvii].

Roberts remained in Gun Trench and on the night of 29th received the fateful news that the Hohenzollern Redoubt had been lost. An order was received that *he* was to recapture it. The implications were grave for the diminished 8th Devons who couldn't possibly succeed in retaking a position that had already cost so many lives. Sensible to the reality Roberts nonetheless complied and led his men through the night in the direction of the redoubt. As he and his second in command attempted to formulate a credible plan of attack a fateful second order came in:

'Hohenzollern still in our hands : 8th Devons will proceed to billets…'[cxxviii], the attack had been cancelled.

Geoffrey Dorling Roberts

Geoffrey Dorling Roberts was born in Exeter in 1886. He first picked up a rugby ball at Exeter School before progressing to Rugby School and then to Oxford. He was given the nickname 'Khaki' after falling in a pile of gravel. A usefully athletic forward, he played for Exeter before Adrian Stoop convinced him to join Harlequins.

In between he represented Devon against the touring All-Blacks in 1905 and Springboks in 1906. The following year he discovered when reading an evening newspaper that he, and six other Devonians, had been selected to play for England against Scotland in a weeks' time.

One of these, Jimmy Peters- England's first black international- scored a try but it wasn't enough to avoid defeat against a strong Scotland side. Danny Lambert joined Roberts in the side against France the following year and England ran out comfortable winners with Roberts himself kicking two conversions. Roberts' final cap came against Wales at Ashton Gate where he kicked another conversion.

Several blues and two Barbarians tours followed before Roberts moved to London and hooked up with Stoop, Poulton and Lambert at Harlequins. His final first class game came during the war when, in 1915, he turned out, alongside Edgar Mobbs, for the Barbarians against a Wales XV.

Having been called to the Bar in 1912 Roberts was made Recorder of Exeter in 1932; and Bristol in 1946. He had a significant role to play at the end of the Second World War when he served as a Prosecutor at the Nuremberg War Trials.

Hohenzollern Redoubt

Hohenzollern Redoubt did indeed fall on the 3rd October and the British were pushed further back toward their original line with 20,000 fewer men. Before then the decimated 8th Devons had been relieved and a familiar face greeted Acting Lieutenant Colonel Roberts during the handover of the position. Douglas Lambert, a fellow Harlequin team-mate of his, who to this day holds an English record of having scored five tries on his international debut, arrived as second lieutenant with Royal East Kent East Regiment (the Buffs) 6th Battalion.

A tall man, Douglas was better known as 'Danny' Lambert, after a famously enormous man who had been exhibited around London a century earlier. The Buffs had been in and out of the trenches over the summer but were now to lead a frontal assault on enemy emplacements on the 13th October. Second Lieutenant Lambert's height would not have helped him as he led his men in a charge towards the same trenches that Roberts' had held a fortnight earlier. As had befallen so many, on reaching the parapet the Buffs discovered that the artillery had failed to cut through the wire. The men were mercilessly gunned down as they attempted to retreat.

Lambert along with twelve other officers and 450 men of all ranks were killed. Like many young men he had married his sweetheart before travelling to France. His son, whom his wife Joyce named Douglas, was born two months after he died.

Danny Lambert

'…about the most dangerous scoring wing that the game has ever seen' - L. Woodhouse[cxxix]

Douglas Lambert was born in South Norwood and attended Cranbrook School, St Edward's in Oxford and Eastbourne College. Big and strong he earned the nickname Danny and initially played as a forward.

Whilst playing for Harlequins, Adrian Stoop recommended he try out as a three-quarter. Quick and powerful Lambert was likened to a fast moving battleship and the tries soon began to flow. He is reputed to have scored seven against Marlborough Nomads[cxxx] and toured Wales with the Barbarians in 1906.

In 1907 he was selected, alongside fellow Harlequins Stoop and John Birkett, to play for England against France in the opening game of the 1907 international season. In a devastating display of finishing prowess Lambert ran in five tries setting an English record for a debutant that would remain unbroken over 100 years later.

He returned in the same fixture the following year and scored again before playing against Wales and Scotland, against whom he kicked two conversions. He then featured for Harlequins in Twickenham's first ever fixture in 1909 before be reselected for international duty in 1911.

He was amongst the points against Wales and the scored a record 22 points (two tries, two penalties and five conversions) against France, a record that would stand until 1990. He earned the last of his eight caps later that year against Ireland.

Danny Lambert has no know resting place and is remembered on the Loos Memorial, St Edward's School and Eastbourne College Memorials and at Knapton and Mundesley parish churches in Norfolk[cxxxi].

Second Lieutenant Harry Alexander of the Grenadier Guards 1st Battalion arrived amongst the October reinforcements. Without any prior experience of the trenches he found himself thrust into the melee of Loos on the 15th October. Although the battle was nearly over, German artillery was improving. A shell scored a direct hit on Alexander's trench killing him two days later. Cheshire-born Alexander had captained England back in 1902 and was a schoolteacher turned professional singer, reportedly possessing of a 'beautiful baritone voice'[cxxxii]. The War paid scant regard for his achievements and Alexander lost his life after just thirteen days of service

Harry Alexander

Born in Oxton, Birkenhead Harry Alexander attended Bromborough School, Uppingham and then Oxford University. An enormous, destructive forward he quickly demonstrated his merit on the rugby field and earned two blues in between turning out for Birkenhead Park.

He was called up for England in 1900 and made his debut alongside Fin Todd in the back row. A much improved England, who had lost the four preceding matches, defeated Ireland by 15 points to 4, with Alexander kicking a conversion.

In a period of inconsistent selection Alexander was the exception to the rule, selected in seven consecutive international matches. In 1902 he was given the honour of leading out a much-changed England side that included Sydney Coopper and John Raphael. His final game for England came later that year in another victory against Ireland. In 1905 he captained Richmond against Dave

Gallaher's New Zealand.

Away from rugby Alexander was a schoolteacher and a professional baritone singer. He married Jean in 1913 and their daughter Louise was born a year later. He is buried in the Arras Road Cemetery and is remembered on war memorials at Birkenhead Park FC, Richmond FC, Oxford University RFC, Corpus Christi College, Uppingham School, Holy Cross Church, Woodchurch and Birkenhead[cxxxiii].

Shortly after Loos, Captain Mobbs found himself 'hauled over the coals' for having endangered a colonel by braving enemy fire in order to rescue two wounded men[cxxxiv]. Nevertheless his star remained in the ascendant. After being introduced to the King, there were rumours that he might soon to become a major. In a letter to his sister Olive he expressed how much he missed Northampton and thought wistfully of returning to the club for a 'short one'[cxxxv].

Khaki Roberts, after issuing a charge against a man for falling asleep on duty in early 1916, received a summons from 7th Division HQ. His diligence and efficiency in quoting Section 6 (I) (k) of the Army Act had been noted and he was offered a second grade staff appointment to focus on military law. After consulting with his CO he accepted the offer and spent the remainder of the war behind a desk[cxxxvi].

The failure of Loos marked a shift in British strategy. John French was removed as commander of the BEF, to be replaced by General Douglas Haig. Haig believed that the conflict could be won on the western front by a war of attrition. The scene was now set for 1916.

1916

Year of Battles

Lieutenant Dobbs, who had so ably assisted the BEF in their retreat from Mons in August 1914, had been promoted to captain shortly after receiving the French Legion d'Honneur. At the time British communications relied on field telephones that were connected to frontal positions by specially laid cables. The system was compromised in 1915 when the Germans found a way to intercept messages using Moritz listening devices. The Fullerphone was introduced in October 1915 to secure transmissions but signalmen like Dobbs found their work impeded by artillery churning up the earth and cutting the cables. By 1916 Dobbs had reached the rank of brevet major and was mentioned in despatches a second time on New Year's Day. Continued rapid evolution of communications would be crucial as the Great War entered the 'Year of Battles'.

The Second Battle of Champagne had shown German Chief of Staff General von Falkenhayn the inherent advantage of defence in trench warfare and he hoped to use this to his advantage in 1916. Verdun had been a French stronghold for centuries and, like Ypres to the British, had become emblematic of French resistance. Like Ypres it was also exposed to artillery fire from three sides. Knowing how important the town was to French morale Falkenhayn hoped that by taking the Meuse Heights, that overlooked the position, they could train their artillery on the French who would in turn commit large numbers of men to its defence. In this way Falkenhayn hoped to redress Germany's growing numerical inferiority in the western theatre and in so doing 'bleed France white'[cxxxvii].

The very first international rugby player to lose his life in the Great War had been Frenchman Alfred Mayssonnie at the Battle of the Marne. In their grief his Stade Toulouse team-mates had dressed him in their team colours and buried him facing the city. The Battle of Verdun was to be one of the longest and bloodiest in history. By its end a further twelve French internationals had joined Mayssonnie in having made the ultimate sacrifice for their country.

The German attack at Verdun had preceded a planned Anglo-French assault in the valley of the Somme. 41 French and British divisions were set aside for the attack that would commence on the 1st July, but was preceded by the most intense phase of the war at sea.

Jutland

HMS *Lion* had been holed up for repairs on the River Tyne after the action at Dogger Bank in early 1915. The following year she was back at the head of the British Battlecruiser Fleet, who she led out of the Firth of Forth on the morning of the 31st May 1916. They were headed for the mouth of the Skagerrak, the strait that runs between Norway and Denmark. The reason for their embarkation was intelligence gathered by Room 40, which indicated significant German fleet activity.

Vice Admiral Reinhard Scheer had been elevated to commander in chief of the German High Seas Fleet in January 1916 and had brought about a change in German naval strategy. Scheer favoured a bolder 'divide and conquer' approach through which he hoped to pick off isolated British patrols and thus favourably alter the balance of power in the North Sea.

In preparation U-Boats were deployed to monitor the movement of British patrols, mines were laid and zeppelin raids planned but later cancelled due to high winds. Much of this activity was picked up by Room 40, who relayed it to the Admiralty thus presenting Britain with a unique opportunity to engage the High Seas Fleet out of port. British Commander in Chief Admiral Jellicoe, recognising that the time for action had arrived, subsequently moved the Grand Fleet out of its base at Scapa Flow for the first time.

Lieutenant Commander Harrison once more travelled with the *Lion* but Jellicoe too had a current England rugby international on his staff in the shape of WJA 'Dave' Davies, the inspirational fly-half who was on board the Grand Fleet's flagship HMS *Iron Duke* as a lieutenant commander and naval constructor.

The wheels were now in motion on what would become the largest naval engagement in history. The Battle of Jutland would involve over 100,000 men and 250 ships[cxxxviii]. As well as Harrison and Davies, England's first Grand Slam winning captain Norman Wodehouse travelled as gunnery officer on the HMS *Revenge*. Earlier in the war Wodehouse had leapt from his own ship to save the life of a drowning man from another, an act for which he would receive the Royal Humane Society Silver Medal for Bravery. Gunnery Officer Lyon, whose battleship *Monarch* had played a part in the sinking of the first German U-Boat in 1914, travelled with the 2nd Battle Squadron. Amidst the destroyer fleet of smaller ships, Engineer Lieutenant Sydney Coopper was on board HMS *Sparrowhawk*.

Eager to resume hostilities it was the *Lion* and her squadron who made first contact with the enemy at around 14.20 later on the 31st May. Having steamed ahead the squadron found itself outnumbered. Believing that they had engaged an isolated British patrol the German battlecruisers began pounding them with their heavy guns, whilst luring them south to where the larger ships of the High Seas Fleet lay in wait.

At 16.00 *Lion*'s Q-Turret was hit, killing all inside. The ship would have been sunk were it not for the heroism of a mortally wounded major who flooded the ship's magazine from inside the destroyed turret. Having narrowly escaped *Lion* found itself at the mercy of German guns[cxxxix].

At 16.02 HMS *Indefatigable* was hit and sunk with a loss of all but two from 1019 men[cxl].

At 16.25 HMS *Queen Mary* was hit and sunk with a loss of all but nine from 1275 men [cxli].

At 16.30 Beatty sighted the High Seas Fleet for the first time and immediately ordered his fleet to turn 180 degrees and retreat to the north. The High Seas Fleet continued in pursuit unaware that a far superior British force lay over the horizon. By the time *Lion* made sight contact with the British Grand Fleet she had received nine direct hits but nonetheless remained afloat. Once the German High Seas Fleet was in range of Jellicoe's dreadnoughts however the balance of power would pivot in favour of the British.

Just before 18.00 the most advanced German light cruisers were intercepted by an advance British squadron. SMS *Wiesbaden* was disabled and later sunk with a loss of 589 lives.

At 18.00 *Lion* came within sight of *Iron Duke* for the first time and Jellicoe deployed his line of dreadnoughts east in an 80 degree arc that covered six miles and included 24 ships. The German fleet, unaware of their presence, sailed directly into Jellicoe's trap. At 18.30 Jellicoe crossed the German 'T' and brought all his guns to bear on an enemy lit up by the sun, which set in the west[cxlii].

Davies' and Jellicoe's ship the *Iron Duke* landed ten direct hits on SMS *Konig*. The large guns of Lyon's super-dreadnought HMS *Monarch* also scored a direct hit on *Konig*, igniting several charges but failing to explode the magazine before engaging German flagship SMS *Lutznow* which later sank. On board *Revenge*, Gunnery Officer Wodehouse landed five direct hits on SMS *Derfflinger*, destroying her gun turrets, and another on SMS *Von der Tann*. The German fleet was now in mortal peril.

Norman Wodehouse

England's first Grand Slam winning captain was born Norman Atherton Wodehouse in Basford, Nottinghamshire in 1887. He attended the Royal Naval School in Lee-on-the-Solent before entering the Royal Naval College as a cadet in 1902.

A powerful scrummager, sound tackler and useful passer Wodehouse was first selected amongst the forwards for the Royal Navy in 1907, the same year that he reached the rank of sub-lieutenant. His leadership qualities shone through in everything that he did, both on and off the field, and he became a mainstay of the Navy and United Services side in the years before the war.

In 1910 he was selected to play for England against France. England won and Wodehouse had helped his national side to a first outright Championship since 1892. He then played in every round of the 1911 season, scoring a try in a 13-8 victory over Scotland at Twickenham in a side that featured Ronnie Poulton, Ronny Lagden, Len Haigh and

Jack King. His run in the side continued throughout the 1912 season, when he first assumed the captaincy.

The following year England won every championship game, an achievement now known as a Grand Slam. The English pack, with Wodehouse to the fore, was dominant throughout and a tradition of English forward dominance was begun.

Wodehouse remained with the Navy at the war's end and was promoted to the rank of commander. He retired in 1940 having achieved the rank of admiral. Inevitably the Second World War brought Wodehouse out of retirement and he was given command of a convoy, heading south along the western coast of Africa.

The convoy was detected and came under attack from German U-boats. Without hesitation Wodehouse ordered his ships to scatter. His own merchant ship, SS *Robert L Holt* was targeted and sunk by submarine *U-69*. There were no survivors. He is remembered on the Liverpool Naval Memorial and at Gotham Church in Nottinghamshire.

At 19.15 Jellicoe succeeded in crossing the T a second time and the German fleet was pounded, registering 37 hits for only two in return. In a stunning reversal Scheer now sought only to escape[cxliii]. After ordering his destroyers to launch torpedoes at their assailants he ordered his battleships to withdraw into the fading light. Superior armour had kept his ships afloat but German Admiral Hipper later acknowledged that only inferior British shells had prevented disaster[cxliv].

Having forced the German fleet west Jellicoe ordered his fleet to spread out in the hope of cutting them off. The smaller craft comprising the destroyer flotillas then continued the battle at close range throughout the night.

Among them, Lieutenant Engineer Sydney Coopper was ensconced in the engine room of HMS *Sparrowhawk* of the 4th Destroyer Flotilla. He had made seven appearances on the wing for England in the 1900s but his ship would soon become embroiled in some of the most chaotic scenes of the battle. Smaller craft such as *Sparrowhawk* were armed with torpedoes but were acutely vulnerable to attack from larger ships. Below deck 37 year old Lieutenant Coopper was about to experience the longest night of his life.

A half-flotilla of destroyers, including *Sparrowhawk* and led by HMS *Broke* vowed to take the fight to the Germans in the darkness. They had some success, sinking two light cruisers and a pre-dreadnought battleship. *Broke* however was detected by German battleship SMS *Westfalen* and came under heavy fire. Lit up by searchlights and shells *Broke*'s helmsman was killed at the wheel. Slumping lifelessly over it he jammed hard to port and set the destroyer on a collision course with *Sparrowhawk* that neither ship could avoid.

Broke collided with *Sparrowhawk* 'end-on' at 28 knots. The collision threw several men from the bridge of the latter ship onto the deck of the other and the resultant chaos is expressed in reports that both captains, believing their ship to be sinking, ordered their men to abandon onto the other. To make matters worse, a third British destroyer HMS *Contest* then ploughed into *Sparrowhawk*'s aft[cxlv].

Contest at least was unharmed and most of the *Sparrowhawk*'s men evacuated to the *Broke*. *Broke* was eventually prized free and as the ships moved clear the full extent of the damage to *Sparrowhawk* was revealed. She had lost a large section of stern due to the impact of *Contest* and her aft was hanging on by a single plate leaving her in imminent danger of sinking. *Contest* had also jammed *Sparrowhawk's* rudder hard over and although Coopper's engine room had kept her engines working she would only turn in small uncontrollable arcs. Despite her dire predicament her captain and a small contingent of men, including Coopper, remained on board.

Nearby another destroyer, HMS *Tipperary,* was immobilised and on fire and lighting up the night sky thus attracting unwanted attention. The last thing *Sparrowhawk* needed now was close attention from German ships or submarines. Glancing from the stricken deck her remaining crew searched the still waters anxiously. All was calm until 2.00am when the unmistakable shape of a German destroyer approached to within 100 yards of their position. To their relief she left them alone, perhaps deciding that both *Sparrowhawk* and the burning *Tipperary* were as good as sunk. If so they were not far wrong and shortly afterwards *Tipperary* did indeed sink.

The first lifting of the gloom began at 3.30am and with no information about how the battle had gone the wrecked destroyer would be at the mercy of the first ship that came their way.

They did not have long to wait. Soon enough out of the morning mists emerged the looming hulk of a German cruiser, the SMS *Elbing. Elbing* had ten guns to the immobilised *Sparrowhawk*'s one. With stony faces the remaining men on board *Sparrowhawk* began bringing up the last of the ammunition from the magazine in advance of one final, hopeless defence. Understandably the men's conversation turned to descriptions of the afterlife but even before they could bring the gun to bear, as if in answer to their prayers, the crippled *Elding* gently heeled to one side, settled forward, stood on her head and sank beneath the grey waves.

Sub-Lieutenant Wood described the encounter thus:

'We had seemed to be absolutely done, there had seemed to be no hope whatever, and then this happened; you can imagine what we felt like'[cxlvi]

Eventually Coopper, his crew and a handful of survivors from the *Tipperary* were found and brought on board HMS *Marksman*. The astonishing story of the *Sparrowhawk* was later recalled in print by several officers. Coopper himself was mentioned in despatches. His engineers had kept the creaking hull of the

Sparrowhawk afloat long enough for the ship's crew to be rescued. As for *Sparrowhawk*, she found her final resting place on the bottom of the North Sea later that morning.

Sydney Coopper

'Who will ever forget S.F Coopper...' D.R Gent[cxlvii]

In the above quote England scrum half Dai Gent goes on to describe Sydney Frank Coopper's unique ability to wait for an opposing tackler to dive for his legs before leaping over the top of him, a skill he put to good use, scoring two tries in seven international appearances.

Born in Hoo in 1878, Sydney Coopper entered the Royal Naval Engineering College at Keyham before turning out for Blackheath, the Barbarians and Devon. He was first selected for England on the wing, against Wales in 1900. In 1902 he scored against Ireland in a narrow victory at Welford Road in a side that also featured John Raphael and Harry Alexander. Coopper didn't feature again for England until 1905 but scored his second international try that year in the final minute of the game against Ireland at Mardyke in Cork.

After the war Coopper remained with the Royal Navy until 1924. In October of that year he accepted the position of secretary with the Rugby Football Union and remained in post at Twickenham for over 20 years. His retirement was postponed in 1939 with the outbreak of war and it fell on Coopper to keep the home fires burning at HQ until 1947. He passed away in 1961 at the age of 82.

Germany celebrated her 'Victory at Skagerrak' for years after the Battle of Jutland[cxlviii]. Germany had sunk fourteen British ships for a loss of eleven. Losses by tonnage were 110,000 for Britain and 62,000 for Germany, by lives 6094 for Britain and 2551 for Germany[cxlix]. Admiral Jellicoe in particular was criticised for not having pursued the German battleships after their initial onslaught on contact and Vice-Admiral Beatty believed that the chance for a Trafalgar-like victory was lost at Jutland.

But history has revised much of what was initially circulated amongst an over-expectant British public. Winston Churchill defended Jellicoe and his tactics by remarking that he 'was the only man on either side who could have lost the war in an afternoon'[cl]. Jellicoe had twice succeeded in crossing the T at Jutland and although a combination of German armour and poorly designed British shells had kept the German ships afloat many of them were in such a state of disrepair after the battle that British naval sea dominance was decisively maintained. The High Fleet limped back to port and the blockade continued.

Jellicoe was made first sea lord in November 1916 and Beatty became commander in chief of the Grand Fleet. He made HMS *Queen Elizabeth II* his flagship and amongst his staff appointments were Lieutenant Commander Davies, transferred from the *Iron Duke*.

Dave Davies

It is perhaps fitting that the player who did the most to break the Welsh stranglehold on rugby union was himself a Welshman. Born in Pembroke in 1890, William John Abbot 'Dave' Davies had been offered a trial with Wales but instead held on for England[cli].

After attending the Royal Naval School at Keyham, he embarked on a career as a naval constructor. An imaginative fly half who could chip, carry and chase, Davies quickly distinguished himself on the field for Pembroke Dock Harlequins as well the United Services Portsmouth, RNC Greenwich and the Royal Navy.

In 1913 he was selected for England to face the touring Springboks at Twickenham. England suffered a narrow defeat but Davies had played well and kept his place in the side. It was a wise decision on the behalf of the English selectors. In a long international career Davies would never again taste defeat in an England jersey.

In the following match it was his brilliant pass that fed Vincent Coates and delivered England their first victory over Wales in Wales since 1895 and a first ever win in Cardiff. A first ever English Grand Slam followed later that year.

At the end of the 1913 season Davies' Royal Navy half back partnership with Francis Oakeley was replicated at international level for the first time and the same partnership helped England to a second successive Grand Slam the following year.

Davies was still on active service as rugby resumed after the war but returned to the national side to form a new half back partnership with another Royal Navy scrum half Cecil Kershaw. In 1921 Davies was installed as captain and promptly led his side to another Grand Slam in a dominant season. In 1923, his final season, he secured a fourth Grand Slam and signed off his magnificent international career by landing a trademark dropped goal in the final moments of the final game against France.

He passed away in Richmond in 1967 at the age of 76 and is celebrated to this day as one of the finest rugby players ever to pull on an England jersey.

The killing fields of the Somme

With enormous losses on either side the French had succeeded in containing the German advance on Verdun. This encouraged Haig to seek major gains in the upper reaches of the Somme River[clii]. The region however was Germany's best defended position on the western front. The most advanced of her three defensive lines was dug-in 30 feet below a chalk ridge, fortified by machine gun emplacements, through which Allied infantry would have no choice but to advance[cliii]. Haig's intention was to overrun all three German lines on the first day of the battle.

At 7.20am on the 1st July a series of enormous explosions occurred along the German front lines as mines were detonated in advance of zero-hour. The bloodiest day of one of the bloodiest battles in human history had begun.

Of the seventeen divisions that attacked, it is thought that only five entered the German positions, the rest were stopped in no-man's land. Like at Loos in 1915, British artillery had failed to cut the wire and after advancing, slowly and in long lines, across no-man's land troops were mown down in their thousands. Around 100,000 men entered no-man's land that day, of which approximately 60,000 became casualties and around 20,000 were killed. It was 'the greatest loss of life in British military history'[cliv].

Haig's first-day objectives were unmet in almost every sector. One of the very few exceptions was the attack and capture of Montauban by the XIII Corps. There the 30th Division had advanced behind a creeping artillery barrage and succeeded in taking the village by 1.00pm. The 18th Division had then compounded the victory by realising their own objectives by 3.00pm. Contrary to Haig's instruction to walk slowly both had succeeded by crossing no-man's land quickly and capturing trenches before their defenders had had time to man their positions.

At least one English international rugby player took part in the advance on the first day of the Battle of the Somme. In support of 30th Division were the 11th South Lancashire Regiment (St Helen's Pioneers). Amongst their number were the remainder of the 3rd Monmouthshire Regiment, who had been decimated at the Second Battle of Ypres in 1915. Captain Hodges, who had himself been blown up in the battle and had returned to the front with pieces of shrapnel still in his body, was with them.

Hodges' regiment was tasked with making good the gains won by XIII corps and on the evening of the 1st July 1916, as British command began counting their losses, he worked by night at Copse Ravine digging communication trenches across no-man's land and consolidating some of the most advanced positions won by the Allies in the battle so far.

Elsewhere however the situation was far less rosy and Haig's strategy was subtly altered to 'wearing down' the Germans. Away from the main point of assault small actions and raids were also taking place, often at night or first light. The night raids had originally been conceived to ward against the lethargy of 1915 but were now used to divert attention away from the main assault on the Somme.

Captain Robert Pillman had earned his first England cap in the final game of the 1914 season before the outbreak of war. When war broke out Robert enlisted with the Royal Fusiliers 10th Battalion before being gazetted with the Queen's Own (Royal West Kent) Regiment, where he progressed to the rank of captain. In 1916 he volunteered for special operations and was made brigade bombing officer. On one of several raids he is reported as having saved the life of one of his men, who had been gassed, by carrying him back to safety.

On the 9th July 1916 he led a night-raid across no-man's land near to Armentieres. After hours crawling through wire, he and five others made it to the enemy trench parapet where they were spotted. Pillman was shot through the thigh and so ordered his men to retire. This they did, though they brought their wounded officer with them, eventually making it to a shelter. Pillman succumbed to his wounds shortly afterwards. Enormously popular he had reportedly turned down three commissions in favour of the advancement of his friends[clv]. He was unmarried and aged just 23 at the time of his death.

Bob Pillman

'As a tackler R.L Pillman was great, his play being always very, very hard, but never foul…' - C.H Pillman[clvi]

Robert Lawrence Pillman was one of three players to earn their one and only England cap in the final game before the outbreak of war. Pillman however was a name that was already synonymous with English rugby due to the exploits of his older brother Charles Henry (Cherry), a prototype openside flanker who had lit up both the 1913 and 1914 seasons before breaking a leg against Scotland. His brother was called up as his replacement.

Born in Sidcup, Kent Bob Pillman attended Merton Court School and then Rugby School where he developed as a flanker along similar lines to his older brother. After leaving the school he joined a firm of solicitors and would likely have qualified had the war not intervened.

He played his rugby for Blackheath, Kent and London Counties, with whom he defeated South Africa in 1912. He adapted well to international rugby, helping England to a comprehensive victory over France and sharing in the spoils of a Grand Slam. There is every reason to believe that he would have gone on to gain many more international caps as long-term successor to his brother.

He lies in Calvaire Military Cemetery in Belgium and is remembered on memorials at Merton Court, Rugby and Sidcup[clvii].

Sergeant Tommy Voyce of the 2/5 Gloucester Battalion had signed up as an eager, fresh-faced seventeen year old in the spring of 1915. By July of 1916 he and his battalion were with the 61st Division in France to the north of Aubers Ridge, where Harry Berry and several of his fellow Glosters had been viciously repelled the previous year. He took the time to write his first will after witnessing the week-long artillery barrage and opening assault at the Somme, leaving 'the whole of (his) property and effects' to his wife.

On the 19th of July Haig sought to follow up an earlier assault on Bazentin Ridge with an attack at Fromelles. Voyce's 61st Division would attack the German salient alongside the 5th Australian Division. For many involved, Fromelles would be their first taste of the western front. But it was a rout. Outnumbered at least two-to-one, and strafed by artillery on two sides, the Allied troops were easily repelled and suffered four times the losses of the Germans, who later described the assault as 'operationally and tactically senseless'[clviii].

Mercifully Voyce's 2/5 Gloucester Battalion had been held in reserve. Instead of joining the rest of the division they were given the grisly task of retrieving and burying the bodies. It took them three days. Later in the war an exploding shell would cause an ocular haemorrhage that rendered Voyce blind in one eye. The injury didn't hold him back however. After the war Voyce would become established as a mainstay of the English pack through much of the 1920s. The only other injury he would sustain during his period of service came whilst playing football (rugby) in the 'inter theatre-of-war competition' in 1919.

Tommy Voyce

'…Voyce appeared to be straining every nerve, sinew and muscle, and he generally arrived, but only just in time.' - W. J. A Davies[clix]

DOING THEIR DUTY

Born in Gloucester in 1897, Anthony Thomas Voyce attended the old National School in Tewksbury. A versatile footballer, equally at home amongst the forwards as the backs Voyce was selected as a fly-half for England Schoolboys in 1911. At the time of his enlistment he was an auctioneer's clerk.

In his career he played for Gloucester, Cheltenham, Richmond and Blackheath. In 1920 he received his call up to the full England squad, initially as a second-row from where he helped defeat Ireland and Scotland.

From 1921 onwards Voyce featured in every competitive England side for six consecutive seasons. It was a period of unprecedented success during which England secured three Grand Slams in four seasons. Voyce, most frequently deployed in the back row alongside William Wavell Wakefield, scored five tries and became an invaluable member of the team with his tireless running, indomitable spirit and relish of contact, that earned him the nickname the 'Happy Warrior' (or 'Grinning Menace' if you were Welsh).

"A wonderful inspiration to any side" - W.W Wakefield

He earned the last of his 27 caps against Scotland in 1926. Away from the field he was an insurance broker and sports administrator. He was the Gloucestershire representative on the RFU Committee between 1931 and 1971 and was the President of the RFU 1960-61. He passed away in 1980 at the age of 82.

Harold 'Dreadnought' Harrison was a professional Royal Marine who had represented both the Army and Navy rugby sides before being selected for England in 1914. He acquired his nickname 'Dreadnought' from his team-mates in the Navy. A lieutenant, who at times had been temporary captain and major, he had been mentioned in despatches for his role in the African campaign in 1915.

Harrison served with the Royal Marine Artillery, assigned to the South African Artillery. His battery was in France at the start of the Somme Offensive and was deployed in support of the assault on Pozieres on the 23rd July. The artillery batteries, shielded as they were from the direct slaughter of the battlefield, had assumed an almost mechanical discipline in the supply, loading and firing of shells, so that they might deliver their devastation as rapidly as was humanly possible.

Sometime prior to the attack, Harrison climbed up a tree, presumably to locate an enemy target. Instead the enemy located him and adjusted their coordinates. Harrison's tree suffered a direct hit with him still up it. Fortunately he survived. He was awarded a DSO for having twice ventured into enemy territory on reconnaissance missions.

These missions provided crucial data on enemy emplacements and made possible an effective artillery bombardment in advance of the Allied attack on the village of Pozieres. An accurate creeping barrage allowed the Australian 1st and 3rd Brigades to rush the Germans in their trenches and so take the town. Harrison's artillery now became the focal point of the town's defence and despite some of the most ferocious shelling of the whole campaign the Allies held on to their gains. Lieutenant Harrison however was gassed and removed from the front on the 29th July. He was taken to England and later declared unfit to return. For the next two years he served as a gunnery instructor at home.

Wearing Down

'Our artillery never stopped firing day and night, and if they keep it up, they ought to go right through...' – L.A.N Slocock

By the end of July the Allies had inflicted around 160,000 casualties on Germany for the loss of 200,000 of their own. Such appalling figures dwarfed all other British losses in the war so far but there was a stark comfort of sorts to be drawn from the growing superiority in the number of British reserves. Immediately west of Montauban lay the village of Guillemont. Haig gave instructions for 'careful and methodical' attacks to proceed 'without delay' on the 2nd August[clx].

On the 7th August, the famous Liverpool Scottish 1/10th Battalion were waiting in reserve at Talus Boise. The battalion had lost their second-lieutenant, Toggie Kendall, within days of arriving in the trenches the previous year but still held a contingent of international rugby players. Amongst them another former England captain Lieutenant Noel Slocock, a tall, broad-shouldered man, who had proved to be a brilliant forward during eight international appearances between 1907 and 1908. 'It is almost impossible to begin to describe the sights and sounds here...' he wrote in a letter to his mother on the 4th August 1916 '...they baffle description and had I not seen them could never have believed that such chaos could be created by man.'

Despite the death and chaos that raged all around, the men of the 1/10th Battalion remained positive. 'No one here seems to know what is happening but from all accounts the German must have had an awful time of it and they seem more demoralised and ready to surrender than at any previous time in the war' wrote Slocock.

In another letter to his father-in-law he described his men being 'cheery and glad' that they are about to 'have a go at close quarters' but confided an inner fear that he had not shared in the letter to his mother- 'my only regret being on Lena's account' (Lena was his wife) 'I of course have not told her I think it better not to, as it would only worry her and do no good'.

Alongside Slocock was Lance-Corporal Jack King, the farmer from Ilkley, who had initially been rejected as too short when trying to enlist with the Yorkshire Hussars in 1914 but had resolutely refused to budge until his enlistment was accepted. He had spent most of 1915 with the Hussars but had requested a transfer to the Liverpool Scottish in 1916 in order to see more of the action. He would get his wish at the Somme.

On the 8th August the battalion received an order to move into trenches outside Guillemont. They began their march at 8pm and took up positions in the front trenches at 4.00am. After marching all night they were informed that they would attack at once. By now all in uniform knew what awaited them when going over the top but Lance-Corporal King was utterly unflinching in his resolve. In a letter to a friend he even made reference to rugby football serving as the well spring of his own bravery:

'I am absolutely A1 in every way. But one can never tell, and so long as I don't disgrace the old Rugby game, I don't think I mind'[clxi]

At 4.20am Slocock and King went over the parapet and walked through the mist and smoke of a German counter-barrage. They attacked in four waves and some of them succeeded in reaching the German trench where they were surprised by German machine guns that had been brought forward and concealed in shell craters.

'Three times that day did they attempt to take Guillemont, and three times they were repulsed, the flower of the grand regiment going down before the hellish machine gun fire of the Boche.' – R.F Oakes[clxii]

Enveloped in machine gun fire their attack was halted. Neither Lance-Corporal King nor Lieutenant Slocock returned. But we get an inkling of how they conducted themselves through the salutary words of Colonel Jonathan Davidson, who himself was wounded in the assault:

'It was a sad day for football. We can ill spare men like these; but if another game of football is never played in Britain, the game has done well, after two years' Command in the Field, I am convinced the Rugby Footballer makes the finest soldier in the world.[clxiii]'

Noel Slocock

'…one of the greatest forwards who ever played…' - A. A Thomson[clxiv]

Lancelot Andrew Noel Slocock was so called because he was born on Christmas Day in Wootton Wawen in rural Warwickshire in 1886. He studied at Marlborough College and learned to play rugby under the tutelage of F. A Leslie-Jones, who had been twice capped for England in 1895. By 1905 Slocock was playing regularly for Liverpool and

Lancashire.

A tall, imposing forward Slocock relished contact and earned a reputation as a powerful scrummager. He was selected for the North in 1906 before scoring two tries for Lancashire against the touring Springboks. This performance brought him to the attention of the England selectors, who considered him for inclusion in England's upcoming game against South Africa. He was selected but in a quite extraordinary administrative error his invitation to play was sent to Dr Arnold Alcock of Guy's Hospital instead.

Alcock would play only once, the error being corrected in England's next fixture against France in 1907. In this game Slocock made his debut alongside Billy Nanson and Danny Lambert and all three scored tries. Before long Slocock was being described as the natural successor to John Daniell and Sammy Woods.

He scored another try against Ireland in 1907 and a third in his eighth and final appearance, against Scotland, when he had the honour of captaining the side. Who knows how many caps Slocock would have earned had his business commitments prevented him from playing beyond the age of 22.

He married Elinor (Lena) Cook in 1912 and the two of them sailed for America in 1914 with their son Anthony. When war broke out Slocock believed that it was his duty to serve and returned to England so that he might enlist. His body was never recovered. He is remembered on the Thiepval Memorial and on others at Marlborough College, Liverpool Football Club, Birkenhead Park Football Club and

DOING THEIR DUTY

St George's Hall, Liverpool[clxv].

He is the subject of the following poem:

> When in the Rugby scrummage stern,
> The forwards in fine frenzy push,
> And all fifteen with hot zeal burn
> To go ahead with dribbling rush.
> There's always one to take the lead -
> To lower his head and come straight through,
> Such is the hero of my screed,
> The man I introduce to you.
>
> What cares he for the hacks that sting?
> The "purler," or contusion sore?
> What recks he of the tackler's fling
> That topples him right o'er and o'er?
> "Hard pounding", as brave Wellington
> Observed at deathly Waterloo:
> And Slocock, with his jersey on,
> Loves "pounding" contests through and through.

And in the line-out,
watch him spring
Aloft in air to grad
the ball;
"He'll break his
neck! His eye in
sling,
Will surely go!" Oh,
not at all,
For here's no
younker made of wax,
Who'll crumble if
you look at him.
But a stout forward
who attacks
With might and main
and purpose grim.

Against the serried
ranks of Wales
He fights with
courage and elan.
And grand persistence
never fails
This muscular young
Englishman.
A forward for a hard-
fought day -
A player who even
Scots may baulk,
Few rugby fliers can
outplay
This speedy Slocock
of the walk.

The Rector of the Somme

Two days after the failed attack on Guillemont an open air service took place next to the field guns[clxvi]. The chaplain was Rupert Edward Inglis. Inglis had played for England as a forward in 1886 and had been ordained in 1889. When war broke out he took it upon himself to encourage the local men of his parish to commit themselves to the service of King and country. Then, at the age of 51, he himself had enlisted with the Army Chaplain's Department. In a letter to his parishioners in July of 1915 he gave his reasons:

'I have felt that in this great crisis in our nation's history, everyone ought to do what he can to help. I have said this both publicly and privately, but it has been hard to tell people that they ought to leave their homes, to go out into strange new surroundings, to endure discomforts and danger – perhaps to face death – it was hard to tell people that this was their duty and then to remain comfortably at home myself.'

As an army chaplain Inglis would be kept busy on the western front, performing field services, administering to the spiritual needs of the men and, when called upon, reading them their last rites. He had spent the tail end of 1915 working in the casualty clearing stations. Primitive and basic in their medical provision the stations were little more than temporary field positions that moved forwards and backwards with the front line.

His letters home reveal a strong but gentle man, frequently distressed by what he witnessed but always on hand to assist. He had noted the arrival of the first swallows during the 1916 spring and the cuckoos, whose calls reminded him of his home in Kent. His wife's home-made cakes (and his whiskey) which he shared amongst them, made him popular with privates and colonels alike.

He had been removed from the front in advance of the first day of the Somme, but as the battle wore on found himself drawn closer and closer to the fighting. Unsurprisingly he had been adopted as a talisman by his men, who called him 'The Rector' and went so far as to name a trench after him[clxvii].

Another former-England international who had become something of a talisman to his men was Lieutenant Colonel Edgar Mobbs. Since the Battle of Loos Mobbs had been promoted again and was now in charge of his battalion. His wider unit, the 24th Division, had been spared the opening days of the Somme and Mobbs had even found time to swim in the river on the 1st August 1916. Now however the 24th Division were ordered to take up almost the exact same positions outside Guillemont that the Liverpool Scottish 1/10th Battalion had occupied in advance of Slocock and King's doomed assault.

The plan was remarkably similar. On the 18th August, the 24th Division were to launch a frontal assault on the same machine gun positions that had cut up the Liverpool Scottish 1/10th Battalion scarcely a week earlier. A dull rain accompanied the creeping barrage as Mobbs men readied their attack and the outcome was almost identical. Of the three divisions that took part in the assault, only the 24th made any progress but once again enemy machine guns and counter-barrage scythed through their advance and prevented them from realising their objectives.

Mobbs himself was hit by a shell in the act of climbing over the parapet[clxviii]. Though injured, he once more refused to be evacuated. Shortly thereafter it was noted that he was unable to walk and he was brought down the line against his will. By the time he reached the casualty clearing station and the severity of his wounds were discovered he had grown too weak to protest . He was taken to a hospital with injuries to his back, spine and lung[clxix].

The constant stream of wounded men kept Inglis the army chaplain busy and by mid-September his clearing station had pushed past Guillemont and into the crater of a German mine on the outskirts of Ginchy. Here the front-line was constantly shifting. Gains were hard won and German counter-attacks perennially threatened to overrun their position.

On the 17th September owing to a lack of men, Inglis was put in charge of a company of stretcher bearers. The 6th Division, to whom he was attached, had been held up at the Quadrilateral Redoubt in their efforts to reach Guedecourt, and a growing number of men lay wounded on the battlefield. Colonel Murray of the King's Shropshire's Light Infantry had made a point of asking Inglis to remain at the station but as fewer and fewer stretcher bearers returned the Rector's instinct to help got the better of him.

The next day he and a handful of others went over the top to retrieve wounded men from the battlefield. He was first hit in the leg and took shelter in a nearby crater. German artillery had caught sight of him and his co-bearer. A second shell, this time a direct hit, killed them both[clxx].

Inglis was 53. Dozens of men wrote to his widow to let her know of their fondness for the Rector, one describing him as 'a man in a million'. He is thought to have personally saved many lives by his decision to go and retrieve the wounded and had been recommended for a Military Cross (MC).

Rupert Inglis

Born in London in 1863 Rupert Edward Inglis was the youngest son of Sir John Inglis, known as the 'Defender of Lucknow' for his role in the Indian Rebellion of 1857. Rupert attended Rugby School, University College, Oxford and then Ely Theological College before being ordained.

Conforming to the Rugby School blueprint for 'muscular Christians', Inglis earned rugby blues in 1883 and 1884, winning both matches comfortably and scoring a try in the second. The contributions of the tall, solidly built Inglis did not go unnoticed by the 1883 Cambridge captain Charles Marriot, who in 1886 would captain England during Inglis' international debut.

Inglis was 51 when war broke out and so the players he shared a field with are of a markedly different vintage to those with whom he served. His first cap, a victory against Wales at Rectory Field, where he often turned out for Blackheath, was played in the company of such luminaries as prototype fly-half Alan Rotherham, Charles Gurdon and the dashing threequarter Andrew 'Drewy' Stoddart.

In his second game he helped England to victory over Ireland and in his third and final game he helped England avoid defeat and thus retain the Calcutta Cup, at the time still a relatively new invention. England and Scotland shared the spoils and Inglis retired without having tasted defeat.

By 1900 Inglis was rector at Frittenden in Kent. He married Helen that year and the couple had three children, Joan, John and Margaret.

Beloved of many, Rupert Inglis' name is memorialised in more places than any other English player to have fallen in the Great War. These include the Thiepval Memorial, Twickenham Stadium, Rugby School, MCC at Lord's, Blackheath FC, University College at Oxford, Oxford University RFC, All Saints at Aldershot and churches in Leicestershire, Basingstoke and Frittenden[clxxi].

Just two days after Inglis perished another England international arrived. Bath's Vincent Coates had been England's leading try-scorer in the first Grand Slam winning season of 1913 before pursuing a career as a surgeon. He arrived at the bombed out remains of Delville Wood, more often referred to as 'Devil's Wood', on the 20th September with 100 Field Ambulance.

Under persistent artillery barrage he carried out his life-saving work on the casualties who flowed through the station. He was awarded the MC for 'conspicuous gallantry and devotion to duty in action' and for having 'tended the wounded under very difficult circumstances'.

Coates would later be posted to Salonika where his work as a bacteriologist would be put to use fighting against the disease that ravaged the men stationed there. He survived the war and became a Member of the Royal College of Physicians.

Vincent Coates

Vincent Hope Middleton Coates was born in 1889. He attended Monkton Coombe School in Bath, Haileybury College and then Cauis College Cambridge. At the age of nineteen he earned a rugby blue in the 1907 Varsity Match, but suffered a heavy defeat at the hands of an Oxford side, that included Harold Hodges, Frank Tarr and Khaki Roberts.

In 1910 he played his first game for Bath and he was selected for Somerset the following year. A strong, willing runner with considerable power and a vicious hand-off he quickly became a player that opponents feared. His try scoring brought him to the attention of the England selectors and he was picked, along with Cyril Lowe, to play on the wings against South Africa in 1913.

Although England lost that game Coates was singled out for special praise by the Springboks. He retained his spot and went on to feature in every game of England's 1913 5-Nations Championship.

With a try against Wales, three against France and another two against Ireland, he was one of England's stand-out performers in their first ever Grand Slam winning season.

Like Lowe, Coates may have remained in the national set-up for many years but instead he opted to pursue the medical career that eventually led him to the front-line. After the war he specialised in the study of arthritis. He was killed in tragic circumstances in 1934 at the age of 45, after being thrown from a moving train.

War of Attrition

In the two months leading up to the 19th September Britain suffered another 82,000 casualties. Her reward had been a gain of just 3 square miles[clxxii]. Both Haig and Rawlinson were criticised for having authorised overly narrow attacks with insufficient numbers and the failure of Haig's muddled 'un-delayed' yet 'careful and methodical attacks' now warranted a tactical rethink.

The losses at Guillemont, though costly, might have served to help develop tactics for dealing with isolated machine guns[clxxiii]. Generals Julian Byng and Arthur Currie conducted a series of detailed analyses during the second half of the campaign that would result in numerous tactical improvements, such as the use of focused artillery, creeping barrages, counter barrages and decentralised infantry. British ingenuity too was about to play its part with the introduction of the world's first armoured self-propelled weapons.

Tanks, named so as to fool the enemy into believing that they were stationary water receptacles, were sent into battle for the first time on the 15th September at the Battle of Flers-Courcelette, the third and final general assault of the Somme. Within hours the Mark 1s had succeeded in overrunning positions that had previously seemed impregnable. In support of the tanks came the New Zealand Division, who attacked and captured a position called the Switch Line in just 30 minutes.

With them came Brevet Major Robert O'Hara Livesay alongside some of the finest rugby players in the world, including Dave Gallaher, prototype openside flanker and captain of the 1905 All-Blacks, George Sellars and James McNeece.

Livesay had been capped twice as a fly-half in 1898 and 1899. He had earned a DSO during the Boer War and by the time of the Somme was General Staff Officer to Major General Russell, in charge of planning, training, directing and conduct of operations at Flers-Courcelette. He would later receive a great deal of credit for the outstanding performance of his division during the battle.

Robert Livesay

Robert O' Hara Livesay was born in Gillingham in 1876. He attended Wellington College before enrolling at Sandhurst in advance of a career in the Army. During this time he developed as a creative half-back, playing for Blackheath, the Army, Barbarians and Kent.

Like Rupert Inglis he is representative of a slightly different generation to most of those who served in the Great War and played alongside the likes of John 'The Prophet' Daniell and Herbert 'Octopus' Gamlin in his short international career for England.

He was recognised as the finest fly-half in England during the 1897-8 season[clxxiv] but had to wait until the final international game of 1898 before making his debut. His half-back partnership with Arthur Rotherham lit up England's play and helped England to a convincing victory against Wales at Rectory Field.

His second and only other cap came in England's next match, also against Wales, but this time in Swansea and with a very different outcome. Wales, on the brink of their first golden age, ran riot defeating Livesay's England by 26 points to 3 in what was England's biggest defeat on record at the time.

In between his career as a soldier Livesay played county cricket for Kent. He served in the Boer War and was involved in multiple actions including the Relief of Ladysmith. He was mentioned in despatches and made a companion of the Distinguished Service Order (DSO).

During and after the First World War he was awarded the Chevalier of the Legion of Honour, the American Distinguished Service Medal and made a Companion of the Order of St Michael and St George (CMG). He retired from the armed forces in 1920 having reached the rank of Brigadier General. He married Margaret in 1917 and passed away in 1946 at the age of 69.

In support of XV Corps were the Machine Gun Corps. The corps had been founded in 1915 after British command had witnessed first-hand the new weapon's effectiveness in the opening encounters of the war. With 41st Company was Lieutenant Merriam, who had been wounded with the 7th Rifle Battalion at Hooge the previous summer. Now, with the infantry section of the Machine Gun Corps, he was in command of six machine guns in support of 14th Division, who attacked alongside the New Zealand Division towards Flers.

The first day was a resounding success. The German third line of trenches was reached and twice as much territory was gained as had been on the 1st July for half as many casualties. German machine guns that had for so long wrought such havoc rattled impotently off the sides of British tanks like peas off a tin can. At one point during the battle an RFC Pilot Corps famously reported:

'A tank is walking down the High Street of Flers with the British Army cheering behind it'[clxxv].

In truth however British tanks were not yet ready. Churchill decried the early deployment of a weapon that he thought had the power to defeat Germany, 'My poor "land battleships" have been let off prematurely & on a petty scale' he wrote later that day[clxxvi]. Of the 49 Mark 1s committed to Flers only a handful fought and returned.

The following day Lieutenant Merriam and the 14th Division resumed their advance but ineffective British artillery hampered their progress and Merriam's machine guns were called into action to protect the men. Over a period of hours 'with great courage and determination' Merriam was commended for having brought his guns into position through a 'personal disregard of danger'.

The counter-fire was predictably intense and as at Hooge the previous year Merriam was once more wounded, this time very severely, but his small company of machine guns allowed 14th Division to hold their position. He would receive the MC for his endeavour.

Having already transferred from a rifle battalion to the Machine Gun Corps Merriam's experiences at Flers perhaps gave him another idea. During his long period of convalescence he would submit a written request to transfer to the Machine Gun Guards, responsible for the newly developing 'heavy branch'. His request was granted. Merriam would return to the front in 1918, this time as a captain with the Tank Corps.

A few miles west, away from the fighting a wounded lieutenant colonel was belligerently demanding he be released from his bed at a Red Cross hospital in Rouen. Sickly and weakened, after having more shrapnel removed from his body, Lieutenant Colonel Mobbs defied the advice of his doctors so that he could re-join his men. He would be back in hospital before the year was out, but on the 25th October 1916 he travelled to the shell ravaged Vimy Ridge to the delight of his men who loudly proclaimed and 'greatly rejoiced' the return of their seemingly indestructible commanding officer.

More than three months after the first day of the Battle of the Somme the campaign was still not over. The British had captured Thiepval and three lines of German trenches but the Germans had already constructed fourth, fifth and sixth lines and despite considerable evidence to the contrary Haig still hoped that cavalry might achieve a decisive 'breakthrough'.

The final assault would take place at Ancre on the 13th November. There the Fifth Army would seek to push beyond Thiepval and the recently taken Schwaben Redoubt towards Beaumont Hamel and Beaucourt-sur-l'Ancre.

Lieutenant Maynard had been discharged from hospital a year earlier, after partially recovering from the wounds sustained at Gallipoli. Now, though still of tender years, he was nearing the completion of his third calendar year of service. On the night before the attack at Ancre he was back with A-Company of the Howe Battalion, on the left flank of the 63rd Division. A freezing night was spent hidden in the mist of no-man's land with each man contemplating the sunrise. At 5.45am an artillery bombardment would precede a creeping barrage and infantry advance towards three lines of enemy trenches[clxxvii].

At zero hour Maynard and A Company stood and calmly walked through a haze of cordite, mist and bullets. Advancing close to the exposed left flank, they came under enfilade fire from the direction of Beaumont-Hamel. As usual enemy bullets took special pleasure in despatching officers and 22 year old Maynard soon found himself as commanding officer of his company. Despite their difficulties Maynard's battalion succeeded in taking all three trenches in the rapid advance. Soon after they found themselves pinned down and further progress was thwarted. It was several days before the Howe Battalion could make base and assess their losses. There it was noted that the young lieutenant was missing.

Having survived Antwerp and Suez and being shot at Gallipoli, Lieutenant Maynard's luck had finally run out. In his short life he had acquitted himself magnificently as a scholar, a sportsman and a soldier. His death near to Beaumont-Hamel, at the age of just 22, marks him out as the youngest English international rugby player to lose his life to the conflict.

Aftermath

The Battle of the Somme remains one of the bloodiest in history. Britain lost 19,240 soldiers on the opening day alone, as wave after wave of men walked calmly to their grave following orders that, in hindsight, bordered on incompetence. Some of the most painful statistics of the campaign relate to the terrain. For the loss of almost 800,000 men the Allies had succeeded in liberating seven miles of French countryside[clxxviii].

But the Somme, and by extension the First World War, was more about numbers than terrain. At Verdun Germany had set out their intention to 'bleed France white'[clxxix]. At the Somme Haig embraced the same dark principle. Although it wasn't the decisive victory he had hoped for, German morale was so damaged by the reversal at the Somme that they were forced fundamentally to reassess their strategy. The real Allied breakthrough to occur at the Somme was in the development of trench tactical assault work. In time the lessons painfully learned in 1916 would facilitate the breakthroughs of later years.

Bob Pillman, Noel Slocock, Jack King, Rupert Inglis and Alfred Maynard all lost their lives as the campaign raged. Others, such as Cyril Lowe, Edgar Mobbs, Laurence Merriam, Robert Livesay and Harold 'Dreadnought' Harrison, still had a part to play in the years ahead. A sixth English international, Leonard Haigh, also lost his life to double pneumonia as the battle wore on. The introduction of tanks demonstrated the value of innovative British engineering and the Army Service Corps had been responsible for ensuring that Britain maintained its technological advantage. Haigh, a useful mechanic, had been training as an officer cadet at the time of his death[clxxx].

Len Haigh

Leonard Haigh was born in Prestwich, Lancashire in 1880. He attended Sandringham House School in Southport before leaving to find work, initially in the Manchester cotton spinning industry.

He developed his rugby skills as a forward for Manchester Football Club throughout the 1900s. He progressed to captain and was selected for Lancashire. In 1909, at the age of 29, he was chosen amongst the forwards for the North to face England.

The following year, on the eve of the 1910 international season his Rest of England side defeated England and thus stated their case for inclusion in the first team. Haigh and seven others turned out for England's first game at Twickenham, where they defeated Wales for the first time in twelve seasons.

Two further caps followed and Haigh helped England claim the Championship for the first time since 1892. In 1911 Haigh added a further four caps to make seven in total.

In 1912 Haigh married Eudora and the couple had a son called John. Like Edgar Mobbs, Haigh took an interest in the burgeoning motor car industry and it was in his capacity as a mechanic that he contributed to the war effort.

He succumbed to double pneumonia in August of 1916 and is buried in Pott Shrigley churchyard in Cheshire alongside his son who lost his life in the Second World War as a Royal Air Force Pilot Officer[clxxxi]. To this day Manchester RFC award the Haigh Cup annually to their most capped player.

1917

Revolutions: real and avoided

The Year of Battles took a severe toll on the morale of all combatants. In Britain in December of 1916 Herbert Asquith was replaced as Prime Minister by Lloyd George. In the same month General Joffre was replaced as Chief of Staff to the French Army by General Robert Nivelle. French workers had been striking for improved working conditions since mid-1916 and these intensified from January 1917 onwards[clxxxii].

Things were even worse in Russia. The Brusilov Offensive of 1916 had been coordinated to relieve pressure on the French at Verdun and complement the action at the Somme. Over three grueling months Russia had had some considerable success, particularly against the Austro-Hungarians. However the success had come for a loss of almost half a million men and severe food shortages at home.

On the 22nd January 1917 more than 150,000 people took to the streets of Petrograd in protest. In March close to 200,000 workers went on strike[clxxxiii]. The Tsar hoped that the Petrograd Garrison would restore order but instead the guards sided with the protestors and the Duma called on the Tsar to abdicate. Within a year he and his family were no more, and the world's first communist state had been established in Russia.

In Germany too food was scarce. Now in their third year of blockade, ways were sought to redress the imbalance by inflicting the same on Britain. Once again they looked to their U-boats and the result was 'unrestricted' warfare. Abandoning previous conventions that limited attacks to military targets Germany began an all-out assault on British maritime shipping and supply. The result was devastating. Between February and April German U-boats sank almost 2 million tons of British shipping, or the equivalent of more than 700 ships[clxxxiv]. This posed a very real threat to Britain's ability to wage war that was only assuaged with the introduction of the convoy system later that year.

'Unrestricted' war at sea infuriated neutral USA whose own shipping was often targeted. Tensions between America and Germany reached breaking point when British intelligence at Room 40 intercepted three German messages bound for Mexico discussing an alliance in the event of war. Ironically President Woodrow Wilson had been re-elected in 1917 on a ticket that celebrated his success in having kept America *out* of the war but matters now came to a head. Wilson declared war on Germany and her allies on the 6th April 1917.

A sickly Lieutenant Colonel Mobbs had spent the Christmas of 1916 in hospital. In his letters home he expressed his belief, bordering on hope, that 1917 would be the year in which decisive victory might be attained 'I do not think the Hun will stand another year of it, I hope not'. His efforts on the Somme were recognised when he became the recipient of a DSO. By March he was in slightly better health and rugby football was back on his mind. After his battalion won the '73rd Brigade Cup' he requested his sister send him specially engraved medals that he might present to them. 'I should like them as soon as possible (before I am killed.)' he added. Shortly thereafter his men found themselves in badly waterlogged trenches close to the foot of Vimy Ridge[clxxxv].

In the skies above, Britain was struggling to negate the air superiority that Germany had enjoyed twelve months earlier when attacking the French at Verdun. The cumbersome British FE2b two-seater reconnaissance aircraft were at least able to carry machine guns, which provided some defence against German 'Eindeckers' who had initiated the 'Focker Scourge'.

The heavy losses suffered by the Royal Flying Corps in 1916 has led some to speculate that life expectancy for young pilots was a little over two weeks after arrival in France. That however didn't deter Cyril Lowe. By the war's outbreak Lowe had already established himself as one of England's finest ever players and to this day the diminutive wing is counted as one of the game's deadliest finishers.

Lowe's plane, the Farman Experimental 2 was a 'pusher', meaning that he and his observer would sit precariously in the nose of the flimsy canvas and wood aircraft with the engine directly behind his seat and the propeller, mid-fuselage, directly behind the engine, pushing them along. He had already been shot down once in October 1916, but worse was to come in March 1917.

Taken by surprise by a German 'Albatross' single-seater fighter plane Lowe's plane had taken damage before he and his observer even realised they were under attack. Unable to out-manoeuver their aggressor they were strafed a second time and Lowe was shot through the shoulder. Counter-fire from his observer forced the German plane to withdraw but the British plane, with its pilot rapidly losing blood, was in a tight spot.

Against the odds Lowe managed to retain his composure and stay conscious for long enough to land the craft safely in a friendly sector whereupon he was rushed to hospital. His convalescence lasted for a month. Many would have been overwhelmed by the near-death experience but not Lowe. Once recovered, he joined Squadron 28 and retrained as a single-seater fighter pilot.

Over the winter the Germans had constructed a new fortified line of trenches, called the Hindenburg Line, to which they had quietly withdrawn. General Nivelle believed that his artillery was capable of achieving a breakthrough in '48 hours' and persuaded Lloyd George to back him in what would become known as the Nivelle Offensive.

The offensive would take place either end of the Somme salient, with Britain and her Allies attacking in the vicinity of Arras. The 24th Division, with Mobbs and his battalion once more primed and ready, took up forward positions on the night of the 8th April. A mixture of rain, sleet and snow accompanied a massive artillery barrage the next morning, the launching of 2.7 million shells commencing at 5.30am precisely. The 24th Division and Canadian Corps then implemented everything that they had learnt at the Somme and by early afternoon Vimy Ridge was theirs[clxxxvi].

German reinforcements began to arrive the next day but they were too late to wrest back control of the high ground. The 24th Division came under heavy shelling however and Mobbs was hit again, for the third time in as many years, this time in the hand. His second in command and runner were both killed by the shell that hit their trench. As usual Mobbs refused to be evacuated[clxxxvii].

Edgar Mobbs

Edgar Roberts Mobbs was one of six children. His father was an engineer and his mother the daughter of a Northamptonshire shoe maker. Born in Northampton in 1882, he attended Bedford Modern School before embarking on a career in the burgeoning automobile industry.

He had suffered a knee injury in his final year at school which prevented him from playing much sport and was a late bloomer as far as rugby was concerned, preferring mixed-hockey and only turning out sporadically for Olney Rugby Club in his early twenties.

Over time he developed into a tall, strong centre or wing-three quarter with an awkward but effective running gait that proved very difficult for his opponents to counteract. By 1904 he was well known locally and was turning out regularly for Olney, Northampton Heathens and Western Turks.

As he filled out physically he added an accursedly strong hand-off, kicking, throwing and try-scoring to his repertoire and during the 1905-6 season made his debut for Northampton Saints. It didn't take Mobbs long to put his stamp on the Saints and within two years he was club-captain.

In 1908 he was selected to captain the combined Midlands and East Midlands Counties against Australia at Welford Road. His thrusting runs from deep set-up two tries and inflicted on the Wallabies their only defeat against an English side for the duration of the tour.

His exploits were noticed by selectors and the following month he was selected for England to face the Wallabies at Twickenham. He made his debut alongside Francis Tarr and eight others under the captaincy of George Lyon and within three minutes of kick-off Tarr and Mobbs' intricate passing resulted in Edgar's first international try.

He played in every round of the 1909 season and landed further tries against Ireland and Scotland. In 1910 he captained England against France and helped England to a first outright-Championship since 1892.

DOING THEIR DUTY

In 1912 he played the first of several games for the Barbarians. In 1913 at the age of 30 he hung up his boots for Northampton Saints after captaining the side for six years and having amassed a total of 234 caps and 179 tries.

He fell in 1917. He never married and his body was never found. He is remembered on the Menin Gate and has his own personal memorial in Abingdon Square, Northampton. His name is recorded on memorials at Olney, Northampton and Franklin's Gardens. Bedford Modern School named 'Mobbs House' in his honour and there is a road called 'Edgar Mobbs Way' in Northampton[clxxxviii].

The British and Canadian success at Arras was unfortunately not matched by the French, who had attacked at Chemin des Dames on the 16th April. Although the British attack had succeeded in drawing German infantry away from the point of attack the location was ill conceived. Chemin des Dames was one of the best fortified positions in the German line. As Nivelle's much vaunted artillery fell short of German positions, French infantry attempted to storm up a wooded hillside and were hampered in their progress by German machine guns. They had 130,000 men captured, wounded or killed without inflicting a significant 'rupture' in the German line. Nivelle was removed as French commander in chief on the 29th April[clxxxix].

With the French now suffering from high casualty rates and exhaustion the discontent that had already been expressed at home began to spread amongst their ranks. Having lost faith in their command a series of general mutinies began in the wake of the failed offensive. These continued into June with as many as 68 divisions refusing to fight. The task of bringing the men to order fell to General Petain, who had replaced Nivelle as Army Chief of Staff.

He did so via a mixture of conciliation and ruthlessness. There would be no immediate French offensives and men would be given extended leave. There followed 3,427 court-martials in which 554 men were sentenced to death. A degree of mercy was shown and only 49 executions were carried out but these were performed in front of the men who were made to march past the remains of the punished[cxc].

Democratic conventions had given France and Britain the flexibility to purge their leaders in a way that tsarist Russia lacked. But as Russia exited the war, ceding large swathes of eastern Europe to Germany, a democratic power from the west was preparing to intervene on behalf of the Allies.

The Flanders Offensives

The extent of the breakdown in French command was not fully revealed to the British until June of 1917. By then plans for an assault on the Messines Ridge were already in hand. The ridge was one of three that surrounded and overlooked the Ypres Salient. Extensive tunnelling under the ridge had allowed the Allies to construct 21 galleries underneath the German positions[cxci]. At 3.00am on the 7th June 1917 over a million pounds of explosives were detonated just ten minutes after the culmination of a seventeen-day long artillery bombardment. The blast is reported to have been heard in England[cxcii].

With tank support, the New Zealand Division, sections of which were under the command of Lieutenant Colonel Livesay, advanced across Hill 63 towards the village of Messines. Further north Lieutenant John Raphael was with the King's Royal Rifle Corps 18th Battalion, advancing through blast craters close to the St Eloi salient. Raphael had won nine caps as a graceful centre three-quarter and in some ways was an unlikely soldier. A self-described pacifist he was also an early advocate for women's suffrage and had stood as the Liberal candidate in the 1909 Croydon by-election[cxciii].

The mined explosives were never more effective than at Messines Ridge. Although Livesay's New Zealand Division encountered resistance, they had taken two German lines in less than two hours and by 9.00am the entire ridge was in British hands[cxciv]. Lieutenant Raphael and the 41st Division had been held up between the St Eloi road and the ruins of White Chateau before they too reached the summit of the low ridge. In support came the ever present 24th Division with Lieutenant Colonel Mobbs and the Northants 7th.

Having secured the position the sector then came under significant enemy shellfire. Mobbs, yet again, was caught up in it. One piece of shrapnel lacerating the back of his neck and another catching him flat across the heart, causing bruising and pain but mercifully not penetrating his body. He is reported to have lost a lot of blood but stayed with his men[cxcv].

While inspecting the progress of his men Lieutenant Raphael and one other were also hit by a shell. Raphael's first concern was for the welfare of others and it was some time before he admitted that he himself was gravely injured. He died in a casualty clearing station on the 11th June after an unsuccessful operation to remove shrapnel from parts of his upper body[cxcvi].

John Raphael

John Edward Raphael was born in Brussels, Belgium in 1882 before attending Streatham School and then Merchant Taylor's. An all-round sportsman he won fourteen blues in four different sports whilst at St John's College, Oxford and in his four rugby blues he scored tries in three.

His rugby style as a tough tackling, unselfish three-quarter was much prized by his team-mates who benefited from his deep-thinking style and continual drive for self-improvement.

In 1902, at the age of nineteen, he received his international call-up and played alongside Harry Alexander and Sydney Coopper in a useful England side that eventually finished second in the table with two wins.

He returned to the England side in 1905 and faced his sternest challenge as a player in England's first ever international contest against New Zealand where he was selected as one of three half-backs and lined up opposite the irrepressible All-Black captain Dave Gallaher.

The last of his nine caps came in England's first ever international against France, in 1906, which England won by nine tries to two (35-8). In 1910 he was selected as captain of the British Isles touring side (British and Irish Lions) for their tour of Argentina. Raphael played as full-back and his side won every game[cxcvii]. In addition to rugby he played cricket for Surrey and to this day is the only batsman to have scored a double century for Oxford University against Yorkshire[cxcviii].

In 1908 he was called to the bar at Lincoln's Inn and in 1909 he stood as the unsuccessful Liberal candidate at the Croydon by-election. He is buried in the Lijssenthoek Military Cemetery in Poperinge along with his greatest opponent on the rugby field Dave Gallaher, who would lose his life later that year.

John Edward Raphael is also remembered on memorials at Merchant Taylors, Lords, the Oval, St John's College, Oxford University RFC and Lincoln's Inn[cxcix].

Buried in the same Lijssenthoek Cemetery as Raphael and Gallaher is Brevet Major George Dobbs. Dobbs, who at Mons had become the first English international rugby player to see action in the Great War, had been made a temporary Lieutenant Colonel in 1916 and was mentioned in despatches for a third time in May 1917. Since the Somme, Royal Engineers signalmen had made significant progress in communications, introducing the grid cable line that would succeed in maintaining lines of communication in the event of artillery fire.

It was whilst he was prospecting for the laying of a cable trench in support of the newly acquired advanced positions at Messines Ridge that he was hit by a shell. Dobbs, who had so ably assisted in the retreat of Mons, had survived until the penultimate year of the conflict. He succumbed to his wounds in the same casualty clearing station as had his former international team-mate Lieutenant Raphael six days earlier.

One day later another rugby playing Royal Engineer was hit by artillery shell. Like Dobbs, Captain Reginald Pickles was taken to a clearing station. Wounded in the hand, forearm and left shoulder for a time it looked as though he would lose his arm. In the end the surgeon's scalpel was tempered and Pickles lost only his thumb. The amputation didn't hold him back however. He was awarded an MC and in 1922 the thumb-less Bristolian full-back made his full international debut in Dublin, helping England to a win over the Irish.

Reg Pickles

Reg Clarence Werrett Pickles was born in Keynsham, Bristol in 1895. He attended Bristol Grammar School where he represented the school XV and developed into a useful back.

Pickles would later play for Bristol, Clifton and Gloucestershire but when all fixtures were cancelled due to the outbreak of war in 1914 he was just eighteen years of age. At the end of the war he was one of a group of players to be selected for the 'Mother Country', a British Army combination side that would contest the 'Inter-services and Dominions Rugby Championship', better known as the 'King's Cup' of 1919.

In the first game against Australia it was Pickles who played in Welshman Clem Lewis for the Mother Country's only try in a narrow victory. He followed this up with tries against the RAF, Canada and South Africa. The side progressed to the final where they were eventually defeated by New Zealand.

In 1922 Pickles received his first full international call up to play at full-back for England against Ireland. England won 12-3 and two weeks later Pickles earned his second and final cap, helping England defeat France at Twickenham.

Pickles played 244 times for Bristol whom he also captained[cc]. He died in 1978 at the age of 82 and is buried in Weston-super-Mare.

Passchendaele

Despite these individual losses Messines was a resounding success and encouraged Haig to pursue a larger offensive around Ypres later that summer. By capturing the village of Passchendaele Haig hoped to progress in the direction of the Belgian coast where the Allies might curtail the threat of the German U-boat. There was, however, significant disquiet at the proposal, the main objections centring on the need to launch another bloody campaign, with American boots on the ground supposedly imminent.

In the end Lloyd George backed Haig. Zero-hour was set for 3.50am on the morning of the 31st July, after a fifteen-day bombardment that utilised four million shells[cci]. Lieutenant Colonel Mobbs had made his battalion headquarters inside a waterlogged trench in advance of Hill 60, where Fin Todd had been shot two years earlier. Further south Lieutenant Colonel Livesay and the New Zealand Division were forming up on the edge of the front line on the southern extremity of Messines Ridge.

The attack would commence in the dark to prevent German observation from the high ground. It was forecast to rain all day. The New Zealand Division made good progress, driving the Germans out of La Basse Ville and repelling a counter attack in the afternoon to hold the position. Mobbs' 24th Division however was less successful in their efforts to secure the strategically important, but waterlogged, Gheluvelt Plateau. Their difficulties were largely due to misfortune. Lower Star Post, a German pillbox stronghold, fell in between the lines of advance for two battalions. As a result both attempted to outflank it and came under heavy fire. The 7th Battalion Northamptonshire Regiment's problems were compounded by enemy machine gun emplacements that had been brought forward of Jeer Trench and they quickly became 'engulfed by heavy fire'[ccii].

As his men's predicament became apparent Mobbs had to be restrained from leaving his bunker. After another 30 minutes of watching the wounded return he could take no more and scaled the parapet with his second lieutenant. His hunch was that a concealed machine gun must be preventing their progress and so he went off in search of it. Sometime later he found it and ordered his second lieutenant to approach it from the opposite flank whilst he himself launched a frontal assault on the position with hand grenades. He was shot through the neck approximately 30 yards from the gun[cciii]. Thinking only of his usefulness to the campaign he spent his last moments scribbling a note for Battalion HQ detailing the machine gun's exact position. His final scribbled words were 'Am seriously wounded'.

Possibly no man was more emblematic of rugby's contribution to the First World War than Edgar Mobbs. His was a character that would have been as recognisable in rugby clubhouses of today as it was then. Though a natural leader of men, he was also modest and had refused his commission in 1914 in order to learn 'the rules of the game'. His irrepressible skill had seen him rise to a position of command just as his skills on the field had brought him to England colours. He had utter faith in his men and must have felt greatly responsible for them after so many had followed him into colours in 1914. Whilst his own ability and courage was demonstrated repeatedly between 1914 and 1917 he would not tolerate incompetence amongst his equals or superiors and had been reprimanded on more than one occasion on this count. Whilst under enemy fire an officious subaltern had pedantically insisted of him that his reports be written in conventional red ink. In a response that was typical of the man, Mobbs replied 'we are in the front-line trenches and have no red ink. There is, however, plenty of red blood here, so if you would like that instead, please instruct me to use it'[cciv]. Edgar Roberts Mobbs is rightly revered in his native Northampton and the Mobbs Memorial Match takes place annually, in his honour, to this day.

Likely on the same day and on the same battlefield one of Mobbs' international team-mates also fell to the same guns. Arthur Wilson was a forward who had helped Mobbs and England defeat Ireland in Dublin in 1909. Unlike most of his former international team-mates Wilson was a private but had been with the 24th Division, though not in Mobbs battalion, since 1915 and had therefore taken part in all of the same battles and campaigns as Mobbs but as a foot soldier. Like so many others who fell in the Great War almost nothing has ever surfaced about the things that he experienced. The son of a Tyneside wool, skin and hide broker, he was 31 at the time of his death[ccv].

Arthur Wilson

Arthur James Wilson was born in 1886 in Newcastle-upon-Tyne, where his father sold wool, skin and hides. He learned to play rugby and cricket at Glenalmond College in Perthshire and on leaving school joined the Camborne School of Mines in Cornwall. A forward, he was recorded by the school as being a 'fine leader of the pack' and in 1907 he was selected to represent Cornwall.

The following year Wilson helped Cornwall to the final of the

County Championship where they defeated Durham to become the county champions for the first time. Later that year Cornwall were drafted in as the British representative at the 1908 Olympic Games. Though soundly beaten by Australia at the White City Stadium, Wilson returned a silver medalist.

In 1909 Wilson received his first and only call-up to the England team where he lined up alongside Edgar Mobbs and Ronnie Poulton for the match against Ireland at Lansdowne Road, Dublin. England had not won in Ireland since 1895 but this time prevailed 11-5 despite losing all of their other championship fixtures that year.

Wilson travelled the world as a mining engineer in South Africa and tea planter in India before enlisting with the Royal Fusiliers in 1915. He has no known resting place and is remembered on the Menin Gate, Glenalmond College, Camborne School of Mines and Camborne Church[ccvi].

The Allies took eighteen square miles for 27,000 casualties on the first day of the third Ypres campaign[ccvii] but the weather impeded further progress. Unremitting rain overwhelmed field irrigation that had already been disrupted by shelling, turning the battlefield into a quagmire.

Earlier in the year at the Battle of Arras the Scots Guards 12th Battalion had lost their lieutenant colonel. His replacement was John Ritson, a career soldier and a former team-mate of Edgar Mobbs, who had played alongside him as a forward in England's 1910 championship winning side. Ritson had already received an MC and DSO earlier in the war for his contributions as a captain and temporary lieutenant colonel with the Durham Light Infantry. As the rains receded in September of 1917 he would lead his men in the Battle of the Menin Road Ridge.

The battle was initially for the same positions, on the Gheluvelt Plateau, that had proved to be so costly for Mobbs and his men. This time in dry weather and with artillery support they made good the gains. Ritson's men were part of the 9th Scottish Division who sought to advance across the Hanebeek Valley, a morass of water-filled craters and some of the bleakest landscapes of the war. In subsequent German counter-attacks lasting several days, Ritson was awarded the Bar to his DSO for his 'exceptional courage and judgement' in repelling attackers under heavy fire and for holding hard-won positions under exceptional difficulties.

John Ritson

John Antony Sidney Ritson was born in Chester-le-Street, County Durham in 1887. He attended Uppingham School before graduating from Durham University with a degree in mining and surveying.

A large man Ritson distinguished himself as a scrummager and tackler for Northern Football Club and in 1908 was asked to tour Australia and New Zealand with an 'Anglo-Welsh' side that was one of the early precursors of the British and Irish Lions.

Ritson featured eleven times on the tour, scoring three tries and featuring in the opening test-match against New Zealand[ccviii]. Two years later, at the age of 22, he was called up to add ballast to the England scrum mid-way through the 1910 season.

He made his debut alongside Norman Wodehouse and Reggie Hands in a side that also included Harry Berry and was captained by Edgar Mobbs. England defeated France at Parc des Princes and Ritson retained his place in the following game against Scotland in Edinburgh. Against the odds England won again and in doing so claimed their first outright Championship victory since 1892. Ritson was amongst the try-scorers.

He was left out of the side the following year but returned at the end of the 1912 season. He then played in every round of the 1913 season earning England a Grand Slam in the process. In his penultimate match Ritson scored a second international try to help England to a convincing win over Ireland in Dublin.

After reaching the decorated rank of lieutenant colonel, Ritson returned to civilian life after the war and resumed his work as a mines inspector. In 1923 he became the professor of mining at Leeds University and he served in the Second World War as the Director General of Mining Supplies.

The wounds he sustained on the western front are reported to have troubled Ritson for the rest of his life. He retired in 1952 and passed away in 1957 at the age of 70.

Like the Battle of the Somme the Passchendaele offensive was protracted and the following month Lieutenant Colonel Livesay's New Zealand Division crossed the plateau in advance of an assault on the Gravenstafel spur in an action known as the Battle of Broodsiende. With the support of a creeping barrage and artillery bombardment they advanced on the ridge, clearing the morass of the Hanebeek where Lieutenant Colonel Ritson had fought his rearguard action. The division came under heavy fire from German machine gun nests but by nightfall had succeeded in most of their objectives and the action was considered a significant success[ccix].

The Allied achievements at Broodseinde prompted a crisis of morale in the German Fourth Army. Haig was encouraged that another push might break them completely allowing a run on the Belgian coast. But rain intervened[ccx]. A fresh deluge hampered Allied operations for the remainder of the month and the Germans, who were retreating from the mud to drier ground, were able to regroup. The Allies on the other hand would have to bring their heavy artillery through the water and crater-filled battlefields if they wished to make further progress.

Eventually the village of Passchendaele was arrived at and taken by the Allies and the Third Battle of Ypres came to an end. Although the Allies had realised many of their objectives in the campaign it was not celebrated at home. In his memoirs Lloyd George referred to Passchendaele as 'one of the greatest disasters of the war'[ccxi]. At its end the land around Ypres, with its morasses, shattered forests and mud was by far the worst battlefield of the war and its tortured landscapes have cast a shadow for many years over the collective British memory of the Great War.

1918

Spring Offensives

The Russian October Revolution of 1917 transferred power to the Soviets of Workers', Soldiers' and Peasants' Deputies allowing Vladimir Ilyich Ulyanov, otherwise known as Lenin, and the Bolsheviks to take control of Russia. On the 3rd March 1918 the treaty of Brest-Litovsk concluded the terms for peace between Germany and Russia with the latter ceding vast swathes of Eastern Europe, including the Baltic States, Belarus and the Ukraine, to German interests.

The long-awaited collapse of the Russian bear allowed 50 German divisions to be transferred from the eastern to the western theatres of war. At a stroke Germany had achieved numerical superiority on the western front[ccxii]. Plans were quickly drawn up for a first western German offensive since Verdun but time was of the essence. American troops had landed in France in 1917 and although their numbers were initially meagre, moves were afoot to raise as many as 1.3 million men by August 1918[ccxiii].

The German intention was to break the back of allied resistance and, in the words of Chief Quartermaster General Erich Ludendorff, specifically to 'beat the British'[ccxiv]. Operation Michael would be launched over the same ground that the British had fought so hard for during the Battle of the Somme. Its objective was simple- to drive the British into the sea.

Lieutenant Colonel Livesay, who had had such success with the New Zealand Division at both Passchendaele and the Somme, had been redeployed over the winter to the American staff school to assist with the incoming recruits. By spring however he was with the 61st Division who lined up alongside Captain Harold Hodges and the 30th Division in a position north of Ham, to the south of St Quentin.

On the night of the 20th March some of Livesay's men launched a daring night-time raid on the German trenches opposite, taking a number of prisoners some of whom revealed that an attack was imminent.

The advance warning of the German 'Kaiserschlacht', gave the depleted Fifth Army a crucial window of opportunity in which an intermittent bombardment was launched on the enemy positions. It wasn't enough to prevent the coming storm however. To the north at Nurlu Lieutenant Colonel Ritson observed the colossal artillery assault that enveloped Livesay's and Hodges' positions at 4.40am the following morning. Winston Churchill, who was with Ritson's 9th Scottish Division described the scenes thus:

'…it swept round us in a wide curve of red leaping flame stretching to the north far along the front of the Third Army, as well as of the Fifth Army on the south, and quite unending in either direction...the enormous explosions of the shells upon our trenches seemed almost to touch each other, with hardly an interval in space or time...The weight and intensity of the bombardment surpassed anything which anyone had ever known before'[ccxv].

The artillery and gas bombardment lasted for five hours before 76 German divisions advanced on just 28 British. Livesay's and Hodges' divisions lay directly in their path. Within an hour they had overrun every position in the Fifth Army's forward line and Flanders was in danger of encirclement. With his men in considerable disarray Captain Hodges was sent to locate the exact position of their right hand battalion. In so doing he entered a building that had been captured by the advancing Germans. Conflicting reports exist about what happened next but one suggests that Hodges attempted to fight his way back out of the building with a handgun.

Harold Hodges who had been blown up at Ypres in 1915 and come through the first day on the Somme had not survived the initial advances of the Spring Offensive of 1918. At home his mother went through the agony of receiving letters from the front expressing the belief of his colonel that her son was likely taken prisoner. But it was not to be and his body was eventually found several months later. In one of many letters a chaplain remarked that Hodges' 'fine strong Christian character' was admired and respected by men and officers alike.

Harold Hodges

Harold Augustus Hodges, born in Mansfield Wodehouse in Nottinghamshire, was one of six brothers. He attended Roclaveston House School and then Sedbergh School where he became captain of the school's rugby team. On leaving Sedbergh he enrolled at Trinity College, Oxford in 1904.

A tenacious prop forward he gained four consecutive blues for Oxford between 1905 and 1908. In the last of these Hodges was made captain and took the courageous, and slightly infamous, decision not to select Ronnie Poulton amongst his backs[ccxvi]. During this period he turned out regularly for Nottingham and was also selected for Midland Counties.

In 1906 Hodges was called upon to represent England against Wales and then Ireland. For his first cap he joined his club captain Vincent Cartwright in the English pack along with George Dobbs and with John Raphael on the wing. They improved on the previous year's result but not enough to avoid defeat.

By 1909 Hodges had found employment as a master at Tonbridge School. He continued to play rugby for Nottingham and 1st class cricket for Nottinghamshire. His body rests in Roye New British Cemetery. He is remembered at Sedbergh School, Oxford University RFC, Trinity College, Oxford and St Peter's Church in East Bridgeford[ccxvii].

By the 5th April the German line had advanced 20 miles, unravelling all the hard won gains of the Somme offensive of 1916. The first meaningful counter offensive was launched the following day bringing the first part of the campaign to a close. But the German thrust was far from over and three days later they attacked at Flanders.

Battle of Lys

The South African Brigade had been responsible for one of the staunchest defences of the allied line on the first day of Operation Michael. Against overwhelming odds they had stood their ground and fought on until there were few left of their number. Dreadnought Harrison's old artillery unit were there in support and second in command of 73rd siege battery was Captain Reggie Hands a former Manchester, Blackheath, Oxford University and England forward, whose brother, also a rugby-player, was a major in the 162nd siege battery. In the same Heavy Artillery unit was another South Africa born rugby player- acting Lieutenant Frank Mellish.

In early April 1918 the remnants of the South Africa Brigade gathered, along with Lieutenant Colonel Ritson's 12th Battalion Scots Guards, under the banner of the 9th (Scots) Division south of Ypres. The Belgian town had resolutely remained under British control for the duration of the conflict but by now little was left. Long fingers of rubble were all that remained of the medieval Cloth Hall and St Martin's Cathedral. Ludendorff's next assault, Operation Georgette, aimed to capture the town and push the British all the way back to the channel ports but for the second time in little over a fortnight the South Africa Brigade stood in his way.

The Battle of Lys began on the 9th April with an enormous artillery barrage and gas attack. The ensuing waves of German shock troops, or stormtroopers as they came to be known, made rapid progress, forcing several divisions to retreat and capturing the towns of Armentieres and Messines.

Fear now gripped the British High Command in a way not experienced since the aftermath of Jutland. With the British position looking increasingly desperate and defeat now a real possibility, Field Marshall Douglas Haig frantically drafted the following 'backs-to-the-wall' special order to be issued to his men:

'Three weeks ago to-day the enemy began his terrific attacks against us on a fifty-mile front. His objects are to separate us from the French, to take the Channel Ports and destroy the British Army.

In spite of throwing already 106 Divisions into the battle and enduring the most reckless sacrifice of human life, he has as yet made little progress towards his goals.

We owe this to the determined fighting and self-sacrifice of our troops. Words fail me to express the admiration which I feel for the splendid resistance offered by all ranks of our Army under the most trying circumstances.

Many amongst us now are tired. To those I would say that Victory will belong to the side which holds out the longest. The French Army is moving rapidly and in great force to our support.

There is no other course open to us but to fight it out. Every position must be held to the last man: there must be no retirement. With our backs to the wall and believing in the justice of our cause each one of us must fight on to the end. The safety of our homes and the Freedom of mankind alike depend upon the conduct of each one of us at this critical moment.'

The tigerish South African Brigade had responded in exactly the manner that Haig proscribed. On the afternoon of the 10th April they counterattacked and drove the Germans back out of Messines. Overnight they and the rest of 9th Division took the fight to the enemy around the Ypres-Comines Canal.

The fighting was intense and often brutal. Captain Hands was caught up in a phosgene gas attack and was taken away to Boulogne. Lieutenant Mellish, who had won an MC at Ypres in 1916, was shot in leg and he too had to be removed to safety. Messines fell again and the fighting continued until the end of the month but Ypres remained in British hands. Ludendorff's strategic objectives were not realised and eventually, after suffering 120,000 casualties German infantry refused to advance further. A twitching General Ludendorff, defeated in Flanders, now cast his eyes south to the French positions.

Lieutenant Mellish made a full recovery from his wounds and when the war ended would play rugby for Blackheath and the Barbarians before being selected for England in 1921. Later that year he returned to his native South Africa and gained further international caps for the Springboks.

Frank Mellish

Born in Cape Town, South Africa in 1897, Frank Whitmore Mellish would become an icon of South African rugby as well as an English international rugby player. After attending Wynberg Boys' High School, Rondebosch High School and South African College Schools Mellish enlisted with the South African Heavy Artillery whilst still a teenager.

He developed his rugby skills as a tough-tackling flanker or second row with the Cape Town Highlanders Regiment side and at the war's end he was selected for the South Africa side in the 1919 'Inter-services and Dominions Rugby Championship' or 'King's Cup'.

Mellish acquitted himself well and, after turning out for Blackheath, was selected for the Barbarians. The following year he was called up by England as part of a new look side that would contest England's first post-war international fixture.

It was the first of six consecutive caps for England during which time Mellish would play alongside Dave Davies, Tommy Voyce, Sid Smart, Frank Taylor and others who had served in the Great War. In 1920 he scored a try against Ireland in Dublin and in 1921 helped England to their first Grand Slam of the inter-war period.

Later in 1921 Mellish returned to South Africa and was immediately selected as a prop for South Africa's first tour of Australia and New Zealand. There the Springboks defeated New South Wales three times and tied the series with the All-Blacks.

He would captain Villagers RFC for several years and helped develop the unusual tactic of the forwards preserving their energy until the final fifteen minutes of the match before going 'berserk' and generally defeating the opposition[ccxviii].

During World War Two Mellish served as a colonel with the South African Armoured Division. Once the war was over he became a selector and in 1951 returned to Great Britain and Ireland as the team manager with a South African side that defeated all four home nations and France.

Frank Mellish passed away in 1965 at the age of 68. His ashes were scattered at Newlands Stadium, home of Western Province for whom he played.

Captain Hands' health was more gravely affected. Both the Germans and the French had begun using phosgene gas in 1915. Unlike mustard gas it was colourless and emitted a pleasant smell, like freshly mown hay. Its effects however were brutal. Attacking the blood-air barrier in the lungs it slowly asphyxiated its victims. Of the estimated 100,000 deaths attributable to gas attacks in the First World War, around 85% are thought to be attributable to the chemical[ccxix]. Hands was treated in a hospital in Boulogne but succumbed to the effects of the gas on the 20th April. He was 30 years old and unmarried.

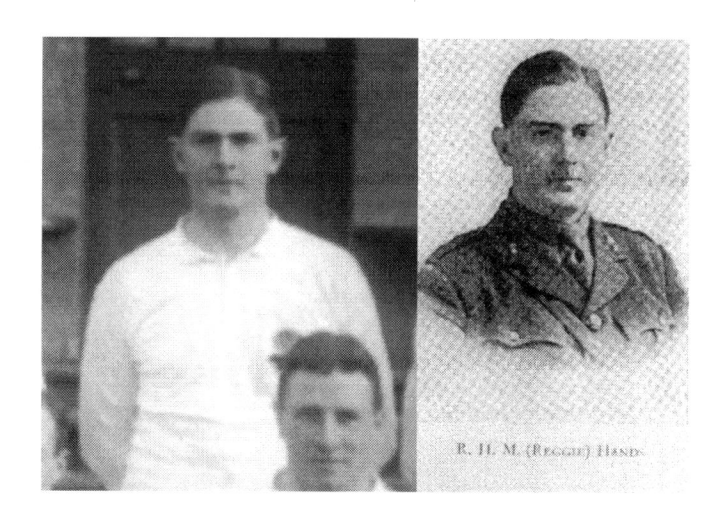

Reg Hands

Reginald Harry Myburgh Hands was born in the suburb of Claremont in Cape Town, South Africa in 1888. He attended Diocesan College in Rondebosch before enrolling at University College, Oxford as a

Rhodes Scholar along with his two brothers Kenneth and Philip.

All three brothers were rugby players and would go on to earn varsity blues. Reggie, a doughty second row forward, was the first and played under the captaincy of Harold Hodges in 1908. The following year he was on the winning side in a team that featured Ronnie Poulton, Ronny Lagden and Frank Tarr.

All three brothers played for Blackheath. Kenneth and Reggie were selected for the Barbarians and in 1909 Reggie was selected in an international trial match for the South against England. The following year he helped 'the Rest' defeat England and forced his way into the England side mid-way through the 1910 season. Wins over Scotland and France helped England to a first outright Championship since 1892 in side that also featured Harry Berry, Edgar Mobbs, Fred Chapman, Norman Wodehouse, John Ritson and Len Haigh.

He became a lawyer in 1911 and in 1914 he and Philip represented the South African cricket team against the touring England side in a test match played in Port Elizabeth.

Captain Hands is buried in Boulogne Eastern Cemetery, Pas de Calais. He is remembered at University College, Oxford University RFC and Blackheath in England and Diocesan College with military memorials at Johannesburg, Kimberley, Cape Town and Port Elizabeth in South Africa[ccxx].

The Flying Winger

At the same time as Field Marshall Haig was issuing his 'backs to the wall' directive in support of the land campaign a feverish contest for air superiority was taking place in the skies. Cyril Lowe, who had been shot down in 1917, returned to France as a captain with 24 Squadron in April of 1918. Now a fighter pilot, Lowe wasted no time in accumulating multiple kills, including a couple of Albatrosses akin to the one that had shot him down the previous year.

In a line of duty that famously had a life expectancy of just seventeen days, Lowe was acquitting himself magnificently as a pilot of the single-seater SE5a. On the 19th May he was appointed escort for a wing of DH4 bombers plotting a raid over Chaulnes. Payload was successfully delivered at 8.15am and the twelve aircraft from 24 Squadron turned and headed back to base. They were soon intercepted by six Fokker tri-planes and seven Fokker bi-planes and enormous dogfight ensued.

One of the British pilots wrote the following account of the engagement:

'soon everyone was busy…planes everywhere, diving, climbing, banking, rolling and falling; some with long plumes of black smoke and flames trailing behind; some on their backs and some on their wing-tips; some in headlong dives. Followed by a tremendous burst of flame. 26 fighter planes trying to destroy each other, 52 machine guns spouting bullets at a rate of 500 or 600 per minute. The crackle of these guns could be heard above the roar of the engines and the shriek of the bracing wires, vibrating at speeds of 150 to 200 mph'[ccxxi].

During the combat Lowe's plane was hit and caught fire. At 17,000ft he dived in an attempt to extinguish the flames. With a Fokker still in pursuit his plane reached

1,500ft. Another plane then distracted the pursuer allowing Lowe to pull up and engage. Between them they defeated the enemy plane and on their return to base both were recommended for MCs[ccxxii].

Engagements such as this and subsequent engagements allowed the Allies to wrest control of the skies. Manfred von Richthofen 'the Red Baron' was shot down and killed during this same period. By the time Germany launched its final desperate attack against the French at the 'second Battle of the Marne' Allied air superiority was complete to the extent that air patrols were able to reconnoitre German infantry movements and so prepare their defence.

In June Captain Lowe was awarded the Distinguished Flying Cross with the following citation:

'This officer has destroyed five enemy planes and driven down two others out of control. On one occasion he attacked two enemy triplanes, although at the time only one of his guns was serviceable; he shot down one of the machines in flames. On another occasion, while leading a formation of eight scouts he engaged a hostile formation of 26 machines. Having shot down a Fokker biplane he went to the assistance of one of our scouts and drove the enemy machine down to 500 feet; at this low altitude half of a blade of his propeller was shot off by fire from the ground.'[ccxxiii]

Cyril Lowe

'…an exceptionally fine wing because of his speed, his initiative, but above all else because of his determination…which largely made him so formidable both in attack and defence.' – W.W Wakefield[ccxxiv]

Born in Holbeach, Lincolnshire in 1891 Cyril Nelson Lowe attended Dulwich College who he represented at boxing, swimming, cricket and rugby. In 1909 he was one of no fewer than five future international rugby players to represent the school XV who duly went through the season unbeaten.

His school nickname was 'Titch' and Lowe was only 5' 6" when turning out on the wing for Cambridge University and Blackheath. His lack of height did not diminish him as a player however and his speed, elusive-running, dangerous cross-field kicking, tackling and try-scoring ability marked him out from an early age.

He earned blues in 1911, 1912 and 1913 and scoring a dropped-goal in the last game, by which time he was already a full international. His debut for England came in 1913 against South Africa at Twickenham. By the end of that year he had helped his national side to their first ever Grand Slam.

In 1914 Lowe scored a total of eight international tries across the season, a record that has never been eclipsed. These included three against Scotland in Edinburgh and another three against France in Paris in a game that delivered England a second consecutive Grand Slam.

He married Ethel in 1915 and became father to two daughters, Alice and Elisabeth. He was acknowledged as a 'Flying Ace' for having shot down five enemy aircraft and his exploits during wartime are believed to have been one of the inspirations behind W.E Johns' fictional character 'Biggles'.

He returned to the national side in 1920 and picked up exactly where he had left-off six years earlier. Two additional Grand Slams were secured in 1921 and 1923 before Lowe retired having amassed 25 consecutive caps and a record eighteen tries.

60 years later Cyril Lowe passed away at the age of 91 with his try-scoring record still intact.

Naval Special Ops- The Zeebrugge Raid

At sea it is possible that Lieutenant Commander Arthur Harrison had grown weary with inactivity. In the early years of the war he had distinguished himself magnificently as a gunnery officer on board Admiral Beatty's former flagship HMS *Lion*. Despite being pummeled within an inch of sinking Harrison had received the DSO post-Jutland for having fired 321 rounds during the engagement. Since Jutland however the stalemate on the seas had resumed and further chances to strike at the enemy had been few and far between.

The Admiralty had not been idle however and the threat posed by German U-boats heightened the need for aggressive naval operations. The top-secret Zeebrugge Raid was one such daring venture. The German occupied Belgian seaports were an ongoing temptation to the Royal Navy who remained in control of the waters around mainland Europe and in January 1918 a plan, put forward by Admiral Roger Keyes, was finally approved.

Zeebrugge's harbour contained the entrance to the Bruges Canal down which German U-boats embarked on their raiding parties. The harbour itself was shielded by a mile-long 'Mole', joined to the mainland by a viaduct. The Grand Fleet was scoured for 'single and athletic' men who might be able to pull of this most daring of raids. Of course Lieutenant Commander Harrison was amongst those who volunteered. Once assembled the men were questioned to ascertain whether they would be willing to take part in 'a hazardous service'. Harrison and all of the other men replied that they would[ccxxv].

The plan was as audacious as it was hopeful. Under the cover of a smoke screen the HMS *Vindictive* and two former River Mersey ferries would approach the mole with

200 marines, who would then storm and secure the enemy gun emplacements. Whilst this was taking place submarines, packed with explosives, would detonate alongside the viaduct, destroying it and preventing enemy reinforcements from coming to the guns assistance. Meanwhile the real objective of the operation would be taking place in the harbour as three obsolete Allied cruisers were floated into the mouth of the canal before being scuttled, thus blocking the embarkation path for the disruptive U-boats.

At midnight on the 22nd April 1918 Lieutenant Commander Harrison was in position outside the bridge on board the HMS *Vindictive* as it floated silently towards the Zeebrugge Mole shrouded in smoke. It would be his responsibility to lower one of several gangways onto the Mole itself, allowing his marines to storm the position. The attack however did not go according to plan. Before *Vindictive* could arrive at the enemy guns the wind changed direction, lifting the smoke-screen and alerting the Germans to their approach. On the Mole twelve large seaward guns, two anti-aircraft guns and a machine gun nest were operated by around 1000 troops[ccxxvi].

At once *Vindictive* came under heavy fire and Harrison, who was in possibly the most exposed place imaginable, was hit in the face by a shell that severely wounded him and killed several others. Concussed, unconscious and with a shattered jaw he was dragged back inside. The severity of the enemy fire then forced the *Vindictive* to land 300 metres further down the mole than planned. Any advance on the enemy would now require marines to cover the exposed parapet on foot and without gun support from *Vindictive*, who was not in a position to bring her guns to bear on the enemy. The marines on board *Vindictive*, HMS *Iris II* and HMS *Daffodil* however were keenly aware that, in spite of these impossible difficulties, the success of the operation depended upon their diversionary attack taking place.

At 12.15 one of the Allied submarines succeeded in destroying the viaduct. Meanwhile Harrison had regained consciousness and though clearly in need of urgent medical attention had proceeded to muster his men in readiness of a frontal assault on the Mole's machine guns. This was the moment for which the self-styled 'death or glory boys' had trained. With cries of 'storm the Mole!!' ringing in the air Lieutenant Commander Harrison and his men then set off on a heroic charge along the parapet and into the face of the enemy guns. Of those that went with him all were killed, bar two who were captured. Harrison himself is reported to have been shot through the neck[ccxxvii]. As he fell to the ground it is possible he might have witnessed the black shapes of HMS *Thetis*, *Intrepid* and *Iphigenia* slip quietly past the Mole into the harbour; and thus known that his own part in the raid had been a success.

Two of the three ships succeeded in scuttling themselves in the mouth of the canal. Consequently the Zeebrugge Raid was initially celebrated as a quite phenomenal success and Admiral Keyes was duly ennobled. Sadly it was a pyrrhic victory at best. U-boats resumed passage of the partially blocked canal just two days later. The heroism and gallant conduct of Harrison and his men was not in doubt however. Eight Victoria Crosses were awarded, one posthumously to Harrison whose actions were later recalled in the *London Gazette*:

'The silencing of the guns on the mole was of the first importance, and though in a position fully exposed to the enemy's machine gun fire Lt Cdr Harrison gathered his men together and led them to the attack. He was killed at the head of his men, all of whom were either killed or wounded. Lieut.-Commander Harrison, though already severely wounded and undoubtedly in great pain, displayed indomitable resolution and courage of the highest order in pressing his attack, knowing as he did that any delay in silencing the guns might jeopardise the main object of the expedition, i.e., the blocking of the Zeebrugge-Bruges Canal.'

Edward Hylton-Young, a gunner, who returned on the *Vindictive* described Harrison as a 'quiet tower of confidence and security'[ccxxviii]. He had played his part well and is the only English international rugby player to have been awarded the Victoria Cross.

Arthur Harrison

Arthur Leyland Harrison was born in Torquay in 1886. He attended Brockhurst Prep School in Shropshire and Dover College before enrolling with the Britannia Royal Naval College in 1901.

A vigorous scrummager with huge strength and tenacious work rate Harrison worked his way through the ranks, playing for the Naval College, Navy and United Services as well as turning out for Rosslyn Park.

He was called up for international duty for the first time in 1914. Selected to play against Ireland at Twickenham he lined up in a front-row that comprised of himself, Alfred Maynard and Dreadnought Harrison. Elsewhere in the side were Cyril Lowe, Fred Chapman, Ronnie Poulton, Dave Davies, Francis Oakeley and Sid Smart.

Harrison was singled out in the press for having done 'three men's work in the scrum' and his play was said to be 'reminiscent of Slocock, Wodehouse, Daniell or Milton'. He was selected again for the final game of the 1914 season and the last before the outbreak of war.

Against France at the Stade Colombes England ran out 39-13 winners with a side bolstered by Mud Dingle and Henry Watson. Once again Harrison was influential and helped his team to a Grand Slam.

Harrison' s final resting place in unknown. He is remembered at Roehampton, St Mary' s Church in Wimbledon, Rosslyn Park FC, Dover College, Brockhurst School and Roundham Head, Paignton[ccxxix].

The Water Hen

Hylton-Young and the battered HMS *Vindictive* eventually made their way back from the assault. A month later *Vindictive* was intentionally scuttled in the mouth of another canal on the Belgian coast, after successfully discharging its duties during the Second Ostend Raid. But her name would not be absent for long from Royal Naval logs. HMS *Cavendish*, initially a heavy-cruiser, was altered in development and launched in 1918 under the name *Vindictive*. This *Vindictive* however was destined to be a wholly new kind of ship, an aircraft carrier.

Shortly after laying anchor in Scapa Flow a 20 year-old flying instructor arrived on the HMS *Vindictive* in advance of a special mission. As a schoolboy William Wavell Wakefield had assisted his uncle in his efforts to devise and build an aircraft that could take off and land on water. They succeeded and for some time Wavell practiced flying the 'Water Hen' across Lake Windermere.

It was only natural then that when he left school in 1916, he would enlist with the Royal Naval Air School. His skill as a pilot was quickly recognised and became a flying instructor at Cranwell, specialising in aerobatics, such as spins, loops and retrieving stalls[ccxxx]. Then, in 1918, a more specialist use was found for his talents.

The usefulness of having a mobile airstrip was apparent to all and the notion of a water-bound aircraft carrier was experimented with in the latter years of the war. At first it was highly debatable whether it was even possible to land an aircraft on a ship. Squadron Commander Edwin Harris Dunning had managed the supreme feat in 1917 but had perished attempting to replicate his landing a second time just five days later[ccxxxi].

It was into this dangerously unpredictable field of experimental flying that young Wakefield was thrust. HMS *Vindictive* had a converted 60 metre landing deck but lacked the arresting gear of later designs. Instead Wakefield would need to bring his Sopwith Pup down at the foot of the runway at a slow enough speed to allow the ship's crew basically to grab hold of the plane and wrestle it to a standstill before it flew off the end of the tiny landing strip and into the waves.

Dunning's fatal crash had been attributed to an updraft disturbing his port wing, precisely the type of turbulence generated by the hot air and smoke streaming from the funnels of the *Vindictive*. The skill required to perform the landing is best described by Wakefield himself:

'We tried to make the task of landing on a ship as safe as possible. But we only succeeded up to a point. The effort that I made was to land successfully by having a fifteen degree angle so that the ship was not steaming directly into the wind, with all the turbulence and hot air and smoke from the mid-ships and funnels coming straight astern.

That would have made it impossible to land, but the changed angle meant that all the disturbed air was going over the starboard quarter. That left the pilot with calm air on the port quarter, and that, in turn made a landing possible, providing there was a speed between 20 and 25 knots available. Anyway, I managed to make the landing.'[ccxxxii]

Though described with casual aplomb such low speeds meant that the Sopwith Pup would have been in danger of stalling for the duration of the landing manoeuver. Wakefield's experience of low level flying in the Water Hen served him well.

William Wavell Wakefield

'In my opinion Wakefield was the greatest forward of all time...'
- John Daniell[ccxxxiii]

Born in Beckenham in 1898 William Wavell Wakefield was nonetheless raised on the banks of Lake Windermere in the Lake District and later attributed his lithe but powerful physique to his childhood spent yomping the Cumbrian Fells.

He attended the Craig School then Sedbergh where he developed as a rugby player with quick, powerful strides and a useful hand-off. The war commenced whilst Wakefield was still at school and he subsequently went directly into the Royal Naval Air Defence. By the time it was over he had helped the RAF side to an unlikely victory over Australia in the 1919 'Inter-services and Dominions Rugby Championship' or 'King's Cup'.

By this time Wakefield had developed into the most complete wing-forward. A sound tackler his powerful running also made him a dangerous attacking outlet and his critical thinking led to numerous tactical innovations in the scrum and line-out. He was also a proponent of the ancient art of dribbling and frequently made use of the wheeled-scrum to initiate attacks.

In 1920 he was selected to play for England for the first time in a team that also included Cyril Lowe, Sid Smart and Frank Mellish. He scored his first try later that year in a match against Ireland at Lansdowne Road. The following year as Dave Davies' pack leader he helped England to a Grand Slam of victories.

They repeated the trick in 1923 before Davies retired and Wakefield was duly installed as captain. Three more victories followed in 1924 and then a fourth against Scotland with Wakefield opening the scoring at Twickenham. Under his leadership England had become the first and so far only side to have achieved three Grand Slams in four seasons. In 1927 he earned his 31st and final cap setting an English appearance record that would stand until the late 1960s.

In between playing for England he played for Cambridge University, Harlequins, Leicester, Neath and Middlesex. In 1939 he returned to active service when world war broke out for a second time and flew several missions for the Royal Air Force. In later life he became the Conservative MP for Swindon and president of the Rugby Football Union. He was knighted in 1944 and ennobled in 1963. He passed away in 1983 at the age of 85.

100 Days Offensive

The German Spring Offensive brought them within 56 miles of Paris before their advance was halted by joint French and American forces. On the 15th July Ludendorff launched 56 divisions against the French. They succeeded in crossing the Marne, but were once again repelled, this time by the French with the assistance of five American divisions.

By now Germany had taken ten times as much land in the Spring Offensives of 1918 as the Allies had taken in the whole of 1917[ccxxxiv]. But they had not 'beat the British' neither had they broken the back of the Allies. And crucially, having lost over a million men at a time when American reinforcements were arriving in force, the campaign had cost them numerical superiority in the field.

The Allies too had taken heavy losses. The South African Heavy Artillery, sans Lieutenant Mellish and Captain Hands, would shortly be bolstered by the return of a familiar face. Dreadnought Harrison had been declared 'unfit' for active service after being shot out of a tree and gassed outside Pozieres in 1916. Now, after two years as a gunnery instructor, Dreadnought was back and would see out the duration of the war with the South Africa Brigade.

Harold Cecil Harrison

The boy that would one day be known as Dreadnought Harrison was born in Solihull in 1889 and attended King Edward's School in Birmingham. On leaving school he enlisted with the Royal Marine Artillery and was selected amongst the forwards for their rugby team.

The classic example of a player adding 'ballast' to the scrum, Harrison's large physical frame and imposing presence was quickly noted and he had assumed the nickname 'Dreadnought' by the time he was selected for the Army, Navy and United Services sides.

Harrison is one of the few players to play for both the Army and the Navy is believed to be the only player to have done so without ever being on the losing side[ccxxxv]. In 1909 Harrison was called up to play for England against Scotland alongside Edgar Mobbs and Ronnie Poulton. The game was a disappointment and Harrison ended up on the losing side and for a time it looked like he was destined to join the ranks of the one-cap wonders.

Five years later however Harrison was reselected after playing for Kent and the Barbarians. Taking his place in a formidable front-row that featured Arthur Harrison and Alfred Maynard, he helped England defeat Ireland at Twickenham. The next match was against old foe Scotland and Harrison demonstrated his considerable technical ability by kicking two essential conversions that delivered England the narrowest of 16-15 victories in Edinburgh.

In the final match of the 1914 campaign Harrison was once again on the winning side, 39-13 this time against France in Paris in a win that delivered Harrison and England the Grand Slam. During wartime he continued to play rugby, captaining the Barbarians against a South Africa Services side in 1915.

After the war Harrison continued his career with the military eventually reaching the rank of Brigadier. He received the Order of the Sacred Treasure of Japan in 1926 and the Order of the Bath in 1939. He died the following year at his home in London at the age of 51.

Also returning to the western front was acting Major Laurence Merriam, who had been wounded in 1915 with 7th Rifle Brigade, before being severely wounded during the Battle of the Somme with the Machine Gun Corps. His actions at the Battle of Flers-Courcelette had earned him the MC. An extended period of convalescence had followed during which time he submitted a hand-written request that he be transferred to the Heavy Branch of the Machine Gun Corps. By August 1918

Merriam was back in France as commander of 'A' Company of the 7th Tank Battalion.

The tanks were the Allies not-so-secret weapon. By now the Mark 1s had been replaced by the more reliable Mark IV and Mark V models. As Major Merriam took his place at the start of what would become known as the Hundred Days Offensive, Britain alone had over 500 medium Mark IVs and Mark V tanks as well as numerous lighter tanks, called 'Whippets'[ccxxxvi]. These latter machines were highly mobile and expected to wreak havoc in the gaps left by the slower models. When the time came the tank companies would lead the assault on the Hindenburg Line, as they had done so with fleeting success at the Battle of Cambrai in 1917. Merriam, as commander of 'A' company, would have up to 24 Mark IV heavy tanks at his personal disposal.

The Allies also planned to make full use of their command of the skies. Infantry divisions would be protected from the air by eight single-seater fighter squadrons who would engage in low combat strafing and bombing as the troops advanced over land. Cyril Lowe and 24 Squadron were attached to the Canadian Corps south of the River Somme and Lowe himself was given command of 'B' Flight.

In August 1918, with fighting machines on the ground and in the air, the British Army was unrecognisable from the expeditionary force that had first set foot on French soil in 1914. With the enemy over-extended, outnumbered and having failed in its main objectives, the time had arrived for the British Army and her Allies to strike back.

The Battle of Amiens would begin on the 8th August 1918, a day that General Ludendorff would later describe as 'the black day of the German Army'[ccxxxvii]. Unlike previous Allied offensives this time there would be no prolonged artillery bombardment. Instead the Fourth Army advanced rapidly, without warning, on German positions. They didn't travel alone however. Overhead Captain Lowe of 24 Squadron ran low-flying bombing runs on the enemy positions whilst to the rear

Major Merriam readied his tanks. In total 324 tanks, including 96 whippets advanced in support of the Canadian Division above whom Lowe kept a close surveillance.

It was a spectacular success. By mid-afternoon they had progressed eight miles, killing, wounding or capturing 50,000 Germans for the loss of only 9,000 of their own[ccxxxviii]. Four additional miles were taken the following day before the advance was halted on the 11th August. This short, sharp, shock was to be the blueprint for further attacks and the initial thrust at the Battle of Amiens inflicted on the Germans their worst defeat since the start of the war.

General Tank

Marshall Foch encouraged Haig to drive home the advantage at Amiens but instead Haig opted to switch the attack before German reinforcements could be brought in to halt their advance. 'A' Company of the 7th Battalion Tank Corps had spent most of 1918 stationed in Lens, north of Arras. Major Merriam now had them assemble north of the River Somme with the 1st Tank Brigade, who were about to lead the advance of the Third Army in the Second Battle of the Somme.

They advanced through a morning mist at 4.55am on the 21st August. On seeing their approach the isolated German infantry, largely cut-off from their artillery, turned and fled. Sterner resistance lay ahead. The Albert-Arras railway line had been transformed into a defensive stronghold with multiple machine gun nests in range of the German defensive guns. It was exactly the type of defensive position that had accounted for so many lives during the opening years of the war but this time, with the assistance of the tanks, things would be different.

Proceeding towards the enemy, each tank was transformed into a swirling cloud of bullets and lead as the German machine guns tried frantically to halt their progress. Undaunted they continued into the maelstrom. Shielded to their rear the ranks of infantry cautiously advanced waiting patiently for their moment to attack.

Of the 190 tanks that took part in the advance 37 suffered direct hits[ccxxxix] but such was the panic sown in the minds of the enemy that the German positions were easily overwhelmed. The town of Albert was captured the following day and by the 2nd September Merriam's battalion had reached and broken through the Drocourt-Queant line, pushing the Germans back to their last defensive stronghold, the Hindenburg Line.

The Hindenburg Line, sections of which ran alongside the St Quentin Canal, comprised deeply dug trenches with concrete bunkers, outworks and defensive works and a support line to the rear. When first constructed in 1916 it had seemed impregnable but now, with tank support, General Rawlinson in particular felt optimistic that it could be decisively breached.

A series of simultaneously occurring, converging offensives were planned to take place along most of the western front on the 26th September. Collectively they would comprise the largest offensive of the war. The British third and first armies attacked towards Cambrai. Once again Merriam's 7th Battalion attacked in support of the Third Army and once again the tanks made the difference.

Their objective on the 27th September was the village of Bourlon but their progress was impeded by the fortified stretch of the Canal du Nord that lay in between. The canal had never been completed and was therefore dry but at up to 50 feet wide and twelve deep it was nonetheless a formidable obstacle for tanks. To compound things the Germans had converted its western bank into a nine foot vertical wall. They had however underestimated the British Mark IVs. Sixteen tanks attacked the canal at Mouvres and all but one succeeded in breaching the earthen defences[ccxl]. The penetration of the canal allowed the British to advance on the village of Boulon, which later fell. With their defensive line breached and seemingly nothing to prevent British tanks from advancing all the way to Berlin the Germans were in a state of disarray.

On the 28th September 1918 German General Ludendorff suffered a nervous breakdown and privately conceded the urgent need for armistice. He attributed the defeat not to the Allied generals but to 'General Tank'.

The Battle of the Canal du Nord was yet another success for the British tank. Major Merriam and the 7th Battalion remained on hand for the remainder of the conflict and would see further action to the west of Cambrai in the final stages of the war. In all they earned six DSO's, 20 MCs, four Distinguished Conduct Medals (DCMs) and 27 Military Medals (MMs).

Laurence Merriam

Laurence Pierce Brooke Merriam's father was an American born into an old settler family from Massachusetts. His business affairs brought him to London and so Laurence was born in Islington in 1894. He attended St Paul's School before enrolling at University College, Oxford. A fit and athletic young man he earned blues for swimming and water polo in 1913 and 1914 and placed in the 50 yard sprint.

Though fast he was also physical and in 1913 he was selected in the second row to play for Oxford University, lining up opposite Cyril Lowe and Alfred Maynard who were representing Cambridge. Merriam was on the losing side on that occasion but may well have been given a second try the following year had the war not intervened.

After the Armistice, despite his wounds, Merriam resumed his first class career playing for Blackheath and Barbarians and in 1920 was selected for England, lining up alongside ten other players making their international debuts against Wales in Swansea. William Wavell Wakefield and Frank Mellish were amongst these with Sid Smart, Jenny Greenwood and Cyril Lowe representing the previous England from side six years earlier. Wales prevailed but bolstered by the return of Dave Davies England would win in Merriam's second and final cap, against France at Twickenham two weeks later.

Merriam had joined the British Xylonite Company in 1919. He spent the rest of his career with the firm, set up by his Grandfather in the 1870s, eventually becoming chairman. During the Second World War he was seconded to the Ministry of Supply and he became a Knight of the Realm in 1949. He passed away in 1966 and the age of 72.

The Armistice

In Salonika Bulgaria opened negotiations for armistice with the Allies on the 29th September. On the 8th October with tank and air support the Allies overran the Hindenburg Line at the Second Battle of Cambrai. The fighting then continued east of the line with Major Harrison providing artillery support to the South African Brigade during the daring recapture of Le Cateau. As the month progressed the Allies closed in on the Mons-Conde Canal and the position that Lieutenant Dobbs had helped the BEF evacuate back in August 1914.

The Armistice of Mudros was concluded on the 30th October bringing a cease to hostilities between the Ottoman Empire and the Allies. The same day the German High Seas Fleet tried to leave port in an attempt to engage Britain at sea a final time but the German crews mutinied. The long British blockade of Germany was now tightening a noose around the Kaiser's neck as food shortages and open revolt took hold of his people.

After encountering stiff Italian, British and French resistance in northern Italy the Austro-Hungarian Empire accepted an armistice on the 3rd November. A German capitulation was now inevitable and shortly afterwards secret negotiations were begun on board a train in the Compiegne Wood. Acceding to all Allied demands Germany agreed to an armistice that would come into effect at 11.00am on the 11th November 1918. Back in Germany Kaiser Wilhelm II abdicated the throne in accordance with Allied demands but also to prevent revolution at home.

Seven days after the final bullets had been fired Reggie Schwarz became the final England international to lose his life to the conflict. Capped three times for England the multi-discipline sportsman had also featured in 20 test cricket matches for South

Africa. In the early part of the war he had served in German South Africa before being transferred to the western front in 1916. There he had earned an MC with the King's Royal Rifles 6th Battalion. He succumbed to illness on the 18th November 1918.

Reggie Schwarz

Reginald Oscar Schwarz was born in the borough of Lewisham in south-east London to a German father and English mother. He attended St Paul's School and then Christ's College, Cambridge where he earned a blue as a half-back in 1893.

He left Cambridge early and continued playing rugby for Old Paulines and then Richmond, who he captained in the 1899-1900 season. In 1899 he was selected at half-back for England against Scotland at Blackheath in a position recently vacated by Robert Livesay.

Though England were not successful during this period Schwarz remained in consideration by playing for Middlesex and the Barbarians. He returned to the national side in 1901 and played alongside Harry Alexander on two occasions.

In 1903 Schwarz went to work on the Johannesburg railway. There he began playing cricket for Transvaal and later South Africa, who he represented in several test matches against England between 1905 and 1912.

He is buried at Etaples military cemetery and remembered at Richmond FC, the London Stock Exchange and Lords' cricket ground.

Somewhere in the region of 1 Million men of the British Empire lost their lives to the Great War. Of them around half were never identified[ccxli]. Those whose bodies were retrieved, such as John Raphael, Ronald Poulton, Robert Pillman, Frank Tarr and Charles Wilson, were buried in one of the many graveyards that now lie scattered across the quiet rural parts of northern France and Belgium. The names of those who were not, such as Noel Slocock, John King, Ronald Lagden, Rupert Inglis, Alfred Maynard and Edgar Mobbs, are recorded on monuments, such as those at Thiepval Ridge and Ypres.

Those who returned bore the scars of the conflict both physically and mentally of the horror that they had witnessed. A few, such as Dave Davies, Jenny Greenwood, Cyril Lowe and Sid Smart were fit enough to return to play international rugby for England once again. Others, such as Frank Mellish, Laurence Merriam, Reg Pickles and William Wavell Wakefield would earn their first caps in the years that followed. Each man had done their duty and for each the notion of representing their country had changed forever.

The fundamentals of rugby union were somehow irrevocably altered by the Great

War. Back in 1895 Sir George Rowland Hill had defended the amateur game with a zeal bordering on mania. For him the gentlemanly principles of amateurism elevated the game above rival football codes and imbued it with a moral and spiritual purity that the others lacked and he was in no doubt that the response of rugby players and clubs when enlisting in 1914 and their subsequent conduct during the war validated this belief.

Others agreed. In the years that followed the Armistice schools up and down England thought carefully about which of the football codes would best mould the character of their pupils and many switched allegiance to rugby union.

Around the world war memorials were erected in an effort to pay tribute to the fallen. Northampton, bereft of her favourite son, sought solace in rugby. The inaugural 'Mobbs Memorial Match' between East Midlands Counties and the Barbarians took place at Franklin Gardens in 1921. Though the teams have changed, the game and continues to this day. In Bristol a public appeal raised thousands of pounds that were used to build a living memorial to the 300 rugby players from the city to have lost their lives in the shape of the Bristol Memorial Ground.

Elsewhere loved ones did what they could to come to terms with their grief. Harriette Raphael had a bronze relief constructed in the image of her son at St Jude on the Hill, Hampstead Garden Suburb. In 1918 she published a collection of his thoughts on rugby and included a foreword in which she wrote:

'The nation has been justified of its children, and the young men whose names were household words a decade ago have played the game in the true sense on the field of battle. They were among the first to go, and wide are the gaps in their ranks. Very gallant gentlemen were those splendid youngsters, veritable sons of the gods, taking with them into the Army that spirit of fair play, that discipline, courage, endurance, and loyalty to leaders they had displayed in their games, when they disported themselves as young Titans.' -Harriette Raphael, 1918.

She never fully came to terms with the loss and in 1929 came to a private agreement with the cemetery keeper at Lijssenthoek that her ashes be buried next to her son's remains. Although illegal the agreement was honoured the following year but remained secret for the following 84 years.

In Yorkshire, moved by the tragedy, loss and survivor's guilt of those who remained, a book- 'In Memoriam' was published in 1919 to the memory of the fallen. In it Yorkshire RFU secretary Bob Oakes, who had earned eight caps for England in the final years of the 19th Century, paid his tribute to the fallen. He had played alongside Charles Wilson, the first English international to lose his life to the conflict, and his final cap coincided with the debut of Reggie Schwarz, the last England international to have perished. He wrote the following:

'…the most exacting, trying, and awful conditions man has ever been called upon to face and to endure. We now know how splendidly the Rugby footballer, in common with every British soldier, fought – aye, and how magnificently he died' – R.F Oakes, 1919.

"LEST WE FORGET"
THOSE WHO PLAYED FOR ENGLAND, SEASONS 1914-15, 1915-16, 1916-17, 1917-18

ABOUT THE AUTHOR

Phil McGowan is the Curator at the World Rugby Museum. He was born and raised in Rochdale. He graduated from University College London in 2007 and joined the Rugby Football Union later that year. He authored *Twickenham; Home of England Rugby* in 2014 and *One Of Us: England's Greatest Rugby Players* in 2015.

@_philmcgowan

---

[i] Various, *Yorkshire Rugby Football Union, in Memoriam 1914-1* p279 (1919)
[ii] O'Brien, *British and American Naval Power: Politics and Policy 1900-1936* p21 (1998)
[iii] Chandler, the Oxford history of the British Army p211 (2002)
[iv] Sewell, *The Rugby Football Internationals Roll of Honour* p30 (1919)
[v] Sewell, *The Rugby Football Internationals Roll of Honour* p195 (1919)
[vi] Chandler, the Oxford history of the British Army p211 (2002)
[vii] Strachan, *First World War: To Arms* p52 (2003)
[viii] Edmonds, *Official History of the War: Military Operations: France and Belgium Part 1* p10 (1937)
[ix] Strachan, *First World War: To Arms* p207 (2003)
[x] Tuchman, *the Guns of August* p231-33 (1962)
[xi] Sewell, *the Log of a Sportsman* p164-165 (1923)
[xii] McLaren. *The History of Army Rugby* p1 (1986)
[xiii] RFU Minutes, 4th September 1914 (1914)
[xiv] Sewell, *The Rugby Football Internationals Roll of Honour* p80 (1919)
[xv] Griffiths, *The Book of English International Rugby* p135 (1982)
[xvi] Sewell, *The Rugby Football Internationals Roll of Honour* p83 (1919)
[xvii] Oakes, *Yorkshire Rugby Football Union, in Memoriam 1914-1* p286 (1919)
[xviii] Sewell, *The Rugby Football Internationals Roll of Honour* p83 (1919)
[xix] Hagger, *Lest We Forget: The 27 England Rugby Internationals who died in the First World War.* p47 (2014)
[xx] Farmer & Hands, *The Tigers Tale* p24 (1993)
[xxi] Farmer & Hands, *The Tigers Tale* p180 (1993)
[xxii] Farmer & Hands, *The Tigers Tale* p24 (1993)
[xxiii] Barron, *Oh When the Saints....* p214 (1993)
[xxiv] Woods, *My Reminiscences* p148 (1925)
[xxv] Woods, *My Reminiscences* p149 (1925)
[xxvi] Collins, *Rugby Recollections* p22 (1948)
[xxvii] Robertson-Glasgow, *46 Not Out* p129 (1948)
[xxviii] Collins, *A Social History of English Rugby Union* p59 (2009)
[xxix] Collins, *A Social History of English Rugby Union* p52 (2009)
[xxx] Various, *Yorkshire Rugby Football Union, in Memoriam 1914-1* p271 (1919)
[xxxi] The Times, 17th November 1914 (1914)
[xxxii] Athletic News, 14th December 1914 (1914)
[xxxiii] Grierson, *Ramblings of a Rabbit* p188 (1924)
[xxxiv] Simkins, *Kitchener's Army: The Raising of New Armies 1914-1916* p104 (2007)
[xxxv] Strachan, *First World War: To Arms* P230 (2003)
[xxxvi] Keegan, *The First World War* p108 (1998)

xxxvii Dougherty, *Land Warfare: From World War I to the Present Day* p16 (2008)
xxxviii Keegan, *The First World War* p107 (1998)
xxxix Hagger, *Lest We Forget: The 27 England Rugby Internationals who died in the First World War.* p23 (2014)
xl Edmonds, *Military operations, France and Belgium 1914-1918.* p326 (1937)
xli Keegan, *The First World War* p137 (1998)
xlii Sewell, *The Rugby Football Internationals Roll of Honour* p231 (1919)
xliii Wilson, *The 1914 Star to the Royal Navy and Royal Marines* p2 (1993)
xliv Sewell, *The Rugby Football Internationals Roll of Honour* p109 (1919)
xlv Edmonds, *Official History of the War: Military operations France and Belgium, 1914 : Antwerp, La Bassée, Armentières, Messines, and Ypres October-November 1914* p35 (1925)
xlvi Edmonds, *Military Operations: France and Belgium: Antwerp, La Bassée, Armentières, Messines and Ypres October–November 1941* p56-61 (1937)
xlvii Sellers, *The Hood Battalion* p21 (1993)
xlviii Wakelam, *Harlequin Story* p54 (1954)
xlix Sewell, *The Rugby Football Internationals Roll of Honour.* p109 (1919)
l Hastings, *Catastrophe: Europe Goes to War in 1914* p354 (2013)
li Strachan, *First World War: To Arms* p197 (2003)
lii Massie, *Castles of Steel: Britain, Germany and the Winning of the Great War at Sea* p146 (2007)
liii Strachan, *First World War: To Arms* p203 (2003)
liv Raphael, *Modern Rugby Football* p114 (1918)
lv Keegan, *The First World War* p287 (1998)
lvi Hagger, *Lest We Forget: The 27 England Rugby Internationals who died in the First World War* p83 (2014)
lvii Gardiner, *Conway's All the World's Fighting Ships: 1906-1921*, p11 (1985)
lviii Hagger, *Lest We Forget: The 27 England Rugby Internationals who died in the First World War.* p83 (2014)
lix McCartney and Bryan, *British Submarines in World War 1* p44 (2008)
lx Thomson, *Rugger My Pleasure* p155 (1955)
lxi Ward, *The Rugby Football Annual 1913-14* p23-4 (1914)
lxii Hagger, *Lest We Forget: The 27 England Rugby Internationals who died in the First World War.* p63 (2014)
lxiii Campbell, *Jutland: An Analysis of the Fighting* (1998) p373-374
lxiv Harris, *Billie: The Neville Letters: 1914-1916* (1991) p203
lxv Cooper, *The Final Whistle: The Great War in Fifteen Players* p66 (2012)
lxvi Stevenson, *1914 1918 The History of the First World War.* p76 (2004)
lxvii Plaster, *The History of Sniping and Sharpshooting.* p293 (2008)
lxviii Giblin, *Bravest of Hearts: The Biography of a Battalion - The Liverpool Scottish in the Great War.* p15 (2000)
lxix Sewell, *The Rugby Football Internationals Roll of Honour.* p80 (1919)
lxx Rugby Football 13th October 1923 p144
lxxi Hagger, *Lest We Forget: The 27 England Rugby Internationals who died in the First World War.* p43 (2014)
lxxii Sewell, *The Rugby Football Internationals Roll of Honour.* P87 (1919)
lxxiii Sewell, *The Rugby Football Internationals Roll of Honour.* P88 (1919)
lxxiv Hagger, *Lest We Forget: The 27 England Rugby Internationals who died in the First World War.* p49 (2014)
lxxv Stevenson, *1914 1918 The History of the First World War.* p157 (2004)

[lxxvi] Cooper, *The Final Whistle: The Great War in Fifteen Players* p68 (2012)
[lxxvii] Walmsley, *The Complete History of the Lions* p34 (2005)
[lxxviii] Hagger, *Lest We Forget: The 27 England Rugby Internationals who died in the First World War* p81 (2014)
[lxxix] Poulton, *Ronald Poulton* p330 (1919)
[lxxx] Corsan, *For Poulton and England* p291 (2009)
[lxxxi] Corsan, *For Poulton and England* p290 (2009)
[lxxxii] Poulton, *Ronald Poulton* p292 (1919)
[lxxxiii] Corsan, *For Poulton and England* p281 (2009)
[lxxxiv] Poulton, *Ronald Poulton* p316 (1919)
[lxxxv] Corsan, *For Poulton and England* p293-294 (2009)
[lxxxvi] Corsan, *For Poulton and England* p297-298 (2009)
[lxxxvii] Poulton, *Ronald Poulton* p323 (1919)
[lxxxviii] Hagger, *Lest We Forget: The 27 England Rugby Internationals who died in the First World War* p69 (2014)
[lxxxix] Thomson, *Rugger My Pleasure* p37 (1955)
[xc] Hodges, letter to mother 22nd April 1915 (1915)
[xci] Hagger, *Lest We Forget: The 27 England Rugby Internationals who died in the First World War* p35 (2014)
[xcii] Sewell, *The Rugby Football Internationals Roll of Honour* p195-196 (1919)
[xciii] Hagger, *Lest We Forget: The 27 England Rugby Internationals who died in the First World War* p79 (2014)
[xciv] Keegan, *The First World War* p216 (1998)
[xcv] Hagger, *Lest We Forget: The 27 England Rugby Internationals who died in the First World War* p17 (2014)
[xcvi] Roberts, *Without My Wig* p105 (1957)
[xcvii] Keegan, *The First World War* p238 (1998)
[xcviii] Keegan, *The First World War* p255 (1998)
[xcix] Stanford Daily, 14th April 1943 (1943)
[c] Keegan, *The First World War* p264 (1998)
[ci] Haythornthwaite, *Gallipoli 1915: Frontal Assault on Turkey* p42 (1991)
[cii] Haythornthwaite, *Gallipoli 1915: Frontal Assault on Turkey* p41 (1991)
[ciii] Gray, *A Military History of Australia* p96 (2008)
[civ] Sewell, *The Rugby Football Internationals Roll of Honour.* p124-125 (1919)
[cv] Hagger, *Lest We Forget: The 27 England Rugby Internationals who died in the First World War.* p63-64 (2014)
[cvi] Sewell, *The Rugby Football Internationals Roll of Honour.* p124 (1919)
[cvii] Hagger, *Lest We Forget: The 27 England Rugby Internationals who died in the First World War* p61 (2014)
[cviii] Hart, *Gallipoli* p384 (2011)
[cix] Crawley, *Climax at Gallipoli: The Failure of the August Offensive* p39 (2015)
[cx] Still, *letter to the Times Newspaper* (1923)
[cxi] Moorehead, *Gallipoli* p244 (2015)
[cxii] Cooper, *The Final Whistle: The Great War in Fifteen Players* p109 (2012)
[cxiii] Cooper, *The Final Whistle: The Great War in Fifteen Players* p110 (2012)
[cxiv] Cooper, *The Final Whistle: The Great War in Fifteen Players* p114-115 (2012)
[cxv] Hagger, *Lest We Forget: The 27 England Rugby Internationals who died in the First World War.* p21 (2014)
[cxvi] Erickson, *Ordered to Die: A History of the Ottoman Army in the First World War* p96

(2001)
[cxvii] Stevenson, *1914 1918 The History of the First World War.* p159 (2004)
[cxviii] Edwards, *Sportsman and Soldier* (1998)
[cxix] Roberts, *Without My Wig* p109 (1957)
[cxx] Roberts, *Without My Wig* p105 (1957)
[cxxi] Roberts, *Without My Wig* p108 (1957)
[cxxii] Roberts, *Without My Wig* p111 (1957)
[cxxiii] Roberts, *Without My Wig* p116 (1957)
[cxxiv] Stevenson, *1914 1918 The History of the First World War.* p159 (2004)
[cxxv] Roberts, *Without My Wig* p111 (1957)
[cxxvi] Keegan, *The First World War* p218 (1998)
[cxxvii] Edwards, *Sportsman and Soldier* (1998)
[cxxviii] Roberts, *Without My Wig* p113-114 (1957)
[cxxix] Woodhouse, *Rugby Football Journal* p579 (1924)
[cxxx] Woodhouse, *Rugby Football Journal* p579 (1924)
[cxxxi] Hagger, *Lest We Forget: The 27 England Rugby Internationals who died in the First World War.* p53 (2014)
[cxxxii] Sewell, *The Rugby Football Internationals Roll of Honour.* p22 (1919)
[cxxxiii] Hagger, *Lest We Forget: The 27 England Rugby Internationals who died in the First World War.* p14-15 (2014)
[cxxxiv] Edwards, *Sportsman and Soldier* (1998)
[cxxxv] Edwards, *Sportsman and Soldier* (1998)
[cxxxvi] Roberts, *Without My Wig* p119-120 (1957)
[cxxxvii] Tucker and Roberts, *World War One* p1925 (2005)
[cxxxviii] Strachan, *First World War: To Arms.* p207 (2003)
[cxxxix] Campbell, *Jutland: An Analysis of the Fighting* (1998) p64-66
[cxl] Campbell, *Jutland: An Analysis of the Fighting* (1998) p60-61
[cxli] Campbell, *Jutland: An Analysis of the Fighting* (1998) p62-64
[cxlii] Massie, *Castles of Steel: Britain, Germany and the Winning of the Great War at Sea* p621 (2007)
[cxliii] Campbell, *Jutland: An Analysis of the Fighting* (1998) p246
[cxliv] Massie, *Castles of Steel: Britain, Germany and the Winning of the Great War at Sea* p671 (2007)
[cxlv] Fawcett and Hooper, *The Fighting at Jutland: The Personal Experiences of Forty-Five Officers and Men of the British Fleet* (1921)
[cxlvi] Fawcett and Hooper, *The Fighting at Jutland: The Personal Experiences of Forty-Five Officers and Men of the British Fleet* (1921)
[cxlvii] Gent, *Rugby Football* p116 (1922)
[cxlviii] Tarrant, V.E *Jutland: The German Perspective- A New View of the Great Battle* p274-6 (1997)
[cxlix] Keegan, '*Jutland*' *MHQ: the Quarterly Journal of Military History* p122 (1989)
[cl] Massie, *Castles of Steel: Britain, Germany and the Winning of the Great War at Sea* p681 (2007)
[cli] Woodhouse, *Rugby Football Journal* p47 (1923)
[clii] Strachan, *First World War: To Arms.* p186 (2003)
[cliii] Robertshaw, *Somme 1 July 1916: Tragedy and Triumph* p31 (2006)
[cliv] Keegan, *The First World War* p317-8 (1998)
[clv] Sewell, *The Rugby Football Internationals Roll of Honour* p148-9 (1919)
[clvi] Sewell, *The Rugby Football Internationals Roll of Honour* p151 (1919)

[clvii] Hagger, *Lest We Forget: The 27 England Rugby Internationals who died in the First World War.* p65 (2014)
[clviii] Duffy, *Through German Eyes: The British and the Somme 1916* p57-58 (2007)
[clix] Davies, *How To Play Rugby Football,* p86 (1933)
[clx] Prior and Wilson, *The Somme* p159 (2006)
[clxi] Sewell, *The Rugby Football Internationals Roll of Honour* p85 (1919)
[clxii] Oakes, *Yorkshire Rugby Football Union, in Memoriam 1914-1* p285 (1919)
[clxiii] Sewell, *The Rugby Football Internationals Roll of Honour* p85 (1919)
[clxiv] Thomson, *Rugger My Pleasure* p38 (1955)
[clxv] Hagger, *Lest We Forget: The 27 England Rugby Internationals who died in the First World War* p77 (2014)
[clxvi] Inglis, *Rupert Edward Inglis, Chaplain to the Forces, Rector of Frittenden* p50 (1920)
[clxvii] Inglis, *Rupert Edward Inglis, Chaplain to the Forces, Rector of Frittenden* p50 (1920)
[clxviii] Grierson, *Ramblings of a Rabbit* p196 (1924)
[clxix] Edwards, *Sportsman and Soldier* (1998)
[clxx] Inglis, *Rupert Edward Inglis, Chaplain to the Forces, Rector of Frittenden* p56 (1920)
[clxxi] Hagger, *Lest We Forget: The 27 England Rugby Internationals who died in the First World War* p39 (2014)
[clxxii] Strachan, *First World War: To Arms.* p188-9 (2003)
[clxxiii] Phillpott, *Blood Victory* p266 (2009)
[clxxiv] Griffiths, *The Book of English International Rugby* p80 (1982)
[clxxv] Farr, *The Silent General: Horne of the First Army.* p126 (2009)
[clxxvi] Gilbert, *Churchill: A Life.* P366 (2000)
[clxxvii] Sellers, *The Hood Battalion* p184-5 (1993)
[clxxviii] Keegan, *The First World War* p321 (1998)
[clxxix] Tucker and Roberts, *World War One* p1925 (2005)
[clxxx] Hagger, *Lest We Forget: The 27 England Rugby Internationals who died in the First World War* p27 (2014)
[clxxxi] Hagger, *Lest We Forget: The 27 England Rugby Internationals who died in the First World War* p27 (2014)
[clxxxii] Strachan, *First World War: To Arms.* p241 (2003)
[clxxxiii] Strachan, *First World War: To Arms.* p235 (2003)
[clxxxiv] Keegan, *The First World War* p379 (1998)
[clxxxv] Edwards, *Sportsman and Soldier* (1998)
[clxxxvi] Strachan, *First World War: To Arms.* p238-9 (2003)
[clxxxvii] Edwards, *Sportsman and Soldier* (1998)
[clxxxviii] Hagger, *Lest We Forget: The 27 England Rugby Internationals who died in the First World War.* p59 (2014)
[clxxxix] Keegan, *The First World War* p353-5 (1998)
[cxc] Smith, *Between Mutiny and Obedience* p206-7 (1994)
[cxci] Prior and Wilson, Passchendaele: The Untold Story p49 (1996)
[cxcii] Keegan, *The First World War* p382 (1998)
[cxciii] Raphael, *Modern Rugby Football* pviii (1918)
[cxciv] Stevenson, *1914 1918 The History of the First World War* p333 (2004)
[cxcv] Edwards, *Sportsman and Soldier* (1998)
[cxcvi] Sewell, *The Rugby Football Internationals Roll of Honour* p159-60 (1919)
[cxcvii] Walmsley, *The Complete History of the Lions* p86 (2005)
[cxcviii] Hagger, *Lest We Forget: The 27 England Rugby Internationals who died in the First World War* p73 (2014)

[cxcix] Hagger, *Lest We Forget: The 27 England Rugby Internationals who died in the First World War* p73 (2014)
[cc] Evans and Atkinson, *The King's Cup 1919,* p67 (2015)
[cci] Keegan, *The First World War* p387 (1998)
[ccii] Edwards, *Sportsman and Soldier* (1998)
[cciii] Edwards, *Sportsman and Soldier* (1998)
[cciv] Grierson, *Ramblings of a Rabbit* p198 (1924)
[ccv] Hagger, *Lest We Forget: The 27 England Rugby Internationals who died in the First World War* p84-5 (2014)
[ccvi] Hagger, *Lest We Forget: The 27 England Rugby Internationals who died in the First World War* p84-5 (2014)
[ccvii] Stevenson, *1914 1918 The History of the First World War.* p334 (2004)
[ccviii] Walmsley, *The Complete History of the Lions* p76 (2005)
[ccix] Liddle, *Passchendaele in Perspective: The Third Battle of Ypres* p 209 (1995)
[ccx] Liddle, *Passchendaele in Perspective: The Third Battle of Ypres* p 209 (1995)
[ccxi] Lloyd George, War Memoirs of David Lloyd George 1917 p435 (1934)
[ccxii] Herwig, *The First World War* p400-1 (1997)
[ccxiii] Harries, *the Last Days of Innocence* p324 (1997)
[ccxiv] Keegan, *The First World War* p423 (1998)
[ccxv] Churchill, *The World Crisis* p768 (1938)
[ccxvi] McWhirter and Noble, *Oxford University Rugby Football Club Centenary History,* p103 (1969)
[ccxvii] Hagger, *Lest We Forget: The 27 England Rugby Internationals who died in the First World War* p35 (2014)
[ccxviii] Difford, *The History of South African Rugby Football,* p61-2 (1933)
[ccxix] Maynard, *Chemical Warfare Agents: Toxicology and Treatment* p447 (2007)
[ccxx] Hagger, *Lest We Forget: The 27 England Rugby Internationals who died in the First World War* p29 (2014)
[ccxxi] Mortimer, *Fields of Glory* p168 (2001)
[ccxxii] Mortimer, *Fields of Glory* p168-9 (2001)
[ccxxiii] Mortimer, *Fields of Glory* p171 (2001)
[ccxxiv] Wakefield and Marshall, *Rugger* p85-6 (1927)
[ccxxv] Corbett and Newbolt, *Naval Operations vol.5* p243 (1931)
[ccxxvi] Cooper, *The Final Whistle: The Great War in Fifteen Players* p231 (2012)
[ccxxvii] Kendall, *The Zebrugge Raid 1918: The Finest Feat of Arms* p109 (2009)
[ccxxviii] Kendall, *The Zebrugge Raid 1918: The Finest Feat of Arms* p211 (2009)
[ccxxix] Hagger, *Lest We Forget: The 27 England Rugby Internationals who died in the First World War* p33 (2014)
[ccxxx] Reason, *Six of the Best* p8 (2004)
[ccxxxi] Guttman, *Sopwith Camel* p30 (2012)
[ccxxxii] Reason, *Six of the Best* p9 (2004)
[ccxxxiii] Thomson, *Rugger My Pleasure* p90 (1955)
[ccxxxiv] Stevenson, *1914 1918 The History of the First World War* p420 (2004)
[ccxxxv] Davies, *How To Play Rugby Football,* p86 (1946)
[ccxxxvi] Keegan, *The First World War* p440 (1998)
[ccxxxvii] Bilton, *The German Army on the Western Front 1917-1918* p73 (2007)
[ccxxxviii] Stevenson, *1914 1918 The History of the First World War* p426 (2004)
[ccxxxix] Fuller, *Tanks in the Great War 1914-1918* p253 (1920)
[ccxl] Fuller, *Tanks in the Great War 1914-1918* p327 (1920)

[ccxli] Keegan, *The First World War* p450 (1998)

Printed in Great Britain
by Amazon